PROPHETIC
Secrets

PROPHETIC Secrets

Learning the Language of Heaven

JENNIFER EIVAZ

Chosen

a division of Baker Publishing Group
Minneapolis, Minnesota

Published by Chosen Books
11400 Hampshire Avenue South
Bloomington, Minnesota 55438
www.chosenbooks.com

Chosen Books is a division of
Baker Publishing Group, Grand Rapids, Michigan

Printed in the United States of America

Library of Congress Cataloging-in-Publication Data
Names: Eivaz, Jennifer, author.
Title: Prophetic secrets : learning the language of heaven / Jennifer Eivaz.
Description: Bloomington, Minnesota : Chosen Books, [2020]
Identifiers: LCCN 2020000823 | ISBN 9780800799212 (trade paperback) | ISBN 9781493424849 (ebook)
Subjects: LCSH: Prophecy—Christianity. | Prophecy—Christianity—Biblical teaching.
Classification: LCC BR115.P8 E58 2020 | DDC 234/.13—dc23
LC record available at https://lccn.loc.gov/2020000823

20 21 22 23 24 25 26   7 6 5 4 3 2 1

I dedicate this book once again
to the Holy Spirit.
He is my powerful Friend
who loves to tell me His secrets,
give me wisdom
and show me the things to come.

Contents

Foreword by James W. Goll   11

Acknowledgments   13

Introduction   15

1. Discovering the Gift of Prophecy   21
2. Prophetic Words Need Prophetic Wisdom   33
3. Perceiving the Prophetic Word   49
4. The Spirit of Wisdom   63
5. Anointed to See   79
6. Wisdom and Secrets for Prophets   95
7. Stay with Ancient Paths   111
8. Wisdom for Visions, Dreams and Signs   127

Appendix: How to Stir Up the Gift of Prophecy   145

Notes   152

Foreword

*O*ur goal is not to be gifted people with influence and a platform but to be the friends of God who come into His council and receive His secrets, which are the language of heaven. Amos 3:7 tells us, "Surely the Lord GOD does nothing, unless He reveals His secret to His servants the prophets." If you come from a traditional cessationist theological background, then you might put a period where there is none. Many wrongly read this verse as "God does nothing." But that is not what this verse describes.

The Holy Spirit is looking for friends with whom He can share the secrets that He hears in His council room in heaven. Deuteronomy 29:29 also gives us insight when it states, "The secret things belong to the LORD our God, but those things which are revealed belong to us and to our children forever, that we may do all the words of this law." So the secret things belong to God. But does He hold them only unto Himself? Proverbs 25:2 gives us another piece to the puzzle: "It is the glory of God to conceal a matter, but the glory of kings is to search out a matter."

Let's unravel this for a moment. One, God has secrets. Two, it is the glory of a king to search out a matter or to discover the secret mysteries of God. Three, secrets are revealed to kingly servants who are friends of God. Four, a culture is then created where God acts on His Word that was once hidden and is now revealed. Amazing!

Remember, this is not a mechanical approach to God but rather a relational intimacy as one friend to another. In your own life, you do not share your secrets with everyone. You share your secrets where there is trust. Trust is not a gift of the Holy Spirit, either. Trust is a commodity of faith, of believing in the One with whom you share your innermost thoughts.

One of my primary life goals is to be become a trustworthy servant-friend of God. I want to be a modern-day John, the beloved, and lean my head upon the chest of the Messiah and hear the pulsating rhythm of the heart of God Himself. I want to feel, sense and know the wind of the Spirit as it moves across the room, a life, a city, a nation. Don't you?

When I first met Jennifer Eivaz, I discerned that I had just met a woman of moral character, one who seeks the face of God and who longs to equip others to do the same. The book that you hold in your hand will help you to unlock the mysteries and secrets of God. Jennifer shares her knowledge of God and offers insight to the wisdom of the ways of God. The fear of the Lord is the beginning of wisdom, and wisdom is to be sought after like a rare jewel. It is priceless. So in a sense, when a person's life is demonstrated through their writings, and it has the spirit of wisdom resting upon it, it is a treasure indeed. And that is what *Prophetic Secrets* is: a treasure chest filled with tools to equip you so that you can wisely go and seek out the once hidden things of God.

With this in mind, it is my honor to compose a foreword for *Prophetic Secrets*. Thank you, Jennifer, for living a life worthy of the cause of Christ and for loving God, your family and the Church so well. We need more prophets and prophetic believers who walk their talk and talk their walk! Well done!

James W. Goll, author, international speaker and founder of
God Encounters Ministries and GOLL Ideation

Acknowledgments

I want to thank my incredible husband and wonderful children for their immense support as I continue to write the books to equip this generation in the supernatural. They have continued to champion me without complaint as I have journeyed through hours of study behind my computer and putting my thoughts into words.

I also want to thank minister and prophet James Goll for obeying the Holy Spirit and giving me the prophetic word that undoubtedly released this book into your hands. In addition, a special thank-you to Kim Bangs at Chosen Books for being attentive to not only hear the prophetic word, but to take the necessary action steps to help bring it to pass.

I always want to thank and not forget Steve Shultz from the Elijah List and Elijah Streams TV for being the initial, divine catalyst for God's plan in my life as a writer. May God continue to bless you, Steve Shultz, with abundance and heaps of blessings (see 2 Chronicles 31:7–10).

Thank you once again, Pastors Brad and Lisa Joss of Paradox Church in Perth, Australia, for your continued friendship and for keeping me company as I wrote yet another chapter on your beautiful shores.

Finally, I want to thank my personal prayer partners who continue to pray selflessly for me and who will read this book. Where would I be without prayer partners like you? You hold up my arms in prayer continuously and keep me ignited for battle.

Introduction

I had just experienced a powerful, life-changing visitation of the Lord. I was in awe of the depth of this precious and holy encounter, which changed my life completely in just moments. I knew I would never be the same. Within hours of this happening, however, an unexpected persecutor rose up against me. Without disclosing the details, I will say that the absolute worst betrayal is when someone in your circle turns on you abruptly.

Over the tense weeks and months that ensued, I happened to be doing a series of online sessions with one of my mentoring groups. The technical coordinator for these sessions had raised the idea to consider minister and prophet James Goll for an online session interview. I knew James hardly at all, having met him just once several years beforehand at a conference. I had read several of his books, though, and enjoyed every one of them. Then we proceeded with an official invitation to James, and he graciously accepted.

As James and I journeyed through the interview, to my utter surprise, he began to prophesy powerfully over my life. First, he began by speaking out a word of knowledge. (A word of knowledge, one of the nine gifts of the Holy Spirit mentioned in 1 Corinthians 12:7–10, is knowing a fact about someone either present or past that you could not possibly know unless the Holy Spirit revealed it to you. The word of knowledge also has the uncanny ability to unleash faith in the recipient to fully receive a prophetic word about the future when they are communicated together.)

In summary, James told the viewing audience my secret prayer that I had been praying for months. I had been praying before the Lord out of Psalm 51:10 that He would "create in me a clean heart," and for no particular reason at the time except that I felt led of the Spirit to pray it over myself. Then he prophesied specifically that I would become one of the "leading trainers of prophetic wisdom in this generation" with a big emphasis on the phrase *prophetic wisdom*.

This prophetic word from the Holy Spirit, now given voice through prophet James Goll, launched the creation of the book that you are reading now. *Prophetic Secrets: Learning the Language of Heaven* is about the supernatural gift of prophecy, the powerful voice of God and the multiple dimensions of prophetic language and spiritual happenings that coincide with it. In this book I explain concepts that normally are not explained or have not been given adequate language for understanding until now.

As for the persecution I had experienced? I do not always understand why things happen the way they happen. I was definitely in a spiritual battle, and the Lord chose to answer my prayers this time by preparing "a table before me in the presence of my enemies" (Psalm 23:5). Unbeknownst to him, not only did James prophesy point for point an opposite word for each accusation, but later in the broadcast he addressed a territorial spirit, specifically a Leviathan spirit, something I had already discerned as the spiritual root of the attack.

Think very carefully through the series of events that took place: first a divine visitation, followed by persecution, which culminated in a prophetic word that ushered in this book that you are reading right now. Also consider the remarkable redemption of God's prophetic ministry in and through my life, given my background in a largely known false religion that boasted in having a superior prophet along with prevailing prophetic revelations.

Growing up in the Church of Jesus Christ of Latter-day Saints, also known as the LDS Church or Mormon Church,[1] I had been taught that the active expression of the gift of prophecy was a sign of the true church and an accessible gift for all believers (referring to Mormons).[2] Although this is biblically true, I do not recall any Mormons prophesying, with the exception of the president of the LDS Church, who, by title and position, is considered a true prophet of God. Be aware that prophetic revelation from an LDS president is given greater authority than the written Scriptures, thus resulting in their highly distorted theology of Jesus,[3] among other false beliefs and so-called revelations and practices. Although I had never worked this out rationally, I had concluded emotionally as a Mormon that only a prophet will prophesy, and a male one at that, as there has never been a female leader of the LDS Church.

My belief structure began to shift slowly, however, following my salvation experience at a small United Pentecostal Church[4] in Los Banos, California. I was a freshman at Modesto Junior College, and this was probably the second time in my life at any mainline Christian church. I had been spiraling out of control, but thankfully I had a zealous uncle who kept inviting my family and me to church.

This particular church service was exuberant and loud in expression, but you could tell by their dress code alone that there were a lot of rules. For example, all the women wore long dresses, let their hair grow long and never wore any jewelry or makeup. The men, on the other hand, kept their hair noticeably short and did not grow any facial hair. In this manner, they believed their outward appearance was a demonstration of inward holiness. I did not know what to think about this, but undeniably Jesus encountered me with His love and power at this peculiar little church, and I was never the same again.

Not only did I surrender my life to Christ wholeheartedly, but I also received the baptism of the Holy Spirit just moments later and began speaking in my heavenly language, also known as speaking in other tongues. The baptism of the Holy Spirit is an authentic biblical experience by which you will receive a brand-new language, only it is a heavenly language and not a natural one.[5] From there, I sought out a church much closer to home that hosted the Holy Spirit but still allowed me to wear makeup and normal clothes.

As I visited a handful of Pentecostal and charismatic churches, I noticed the freedom for both men and women to prophesy, and yet none of them claimed outwardly to be prophets. They were not even in charge of the church! They simply prophesied when the Holy Spirit moved upon them, which was usually during the corporate worship. I also observed that few people prophesied in these churches (usually a small select group of mostly older people). Some of those prophetic words were extraordinary and highly dynamic, while others seemed to fall flat on the floor. I was not sure what made the difference either.

I recognized at the time that I, too, was beginning to hear and see the voice of God for myself and for others, but with mixed results. There was no instruction about this gift, and my revelation seemed to be different in scope and strength than most people around me. And they did not use the terms *seer*, *discerner* or *feeler* back then—all terms we are starting to become familiar with now. I also struggled with knowing how to communicate prophetic words very effectively. Too often, I found myself saying things all wrong or, out of timidity, just keeping my thoughts and impressions to myself.

Several years later, even though I was married and in full-time ministry alongside my husband, I struggled to become more fluent and effective in the gift of prophecy. There was a point where I was also called by the Lord in a vision as a prophet, which is something I will discuss later in this book. Regardless, our church had the same issue that I observed in my beginning years at these other churches. There were just a few people, mostly older folks, in the church who prophesied, and it was almost always during the corporate worship. Their prophetic words had very little life on them, and I kept thinking, *There has to be more to the gift of prophecy than this.*

Eventually, I located some teaching material and announced to my church what I believe was their first-ever training in the gift of prophecy. I was shocked to see over seventy hungry people come out for the twelve-week immersion. Even more surprising was the ease they had in stepping into the gift of prophecy, as well as the accuracy they exhibited almost immediately. Here, I discovered by experience a truth presented in the Bible, namely, "You can all prophesy" (1 Corinthians 14:31).

My decision to equip and activate people in the gift of prophecy was a success. As a result, this supernatural gift became accessible to our church at large, rather than being confined to just a few people. This season of training also revealed the hearts of a few "elite" parishioners who believed they were God's elect prophetic voice to our church—an attitude of pride I did not know was there. The accuracy that I mentioned seemed unusual to me, but we had built into our culture some key ingredients that helped foster it, namely childlike faith in the supernatural and a passion for God's written Word.

Dear reader, I exhort you to take deeply to heart what you are about to receive from these chapters. And I pray that the gift of prophecy will be awakened in you, specifically its origins and foundations, as you grow in your awareness of the thoughts, principles and wisdom that shape the many dimensions of prophetic ministry. The prophetic secrets inscribed here are for you, and appropriately so, all because of a word of prophecy.

One

Discovering the Gift
of Prophecy

I did not mean to prophesy. The words just spilled out of my mouth before I knew what was happening. I was two years old in the Lord, about age twenty, and soaking up the heaven-infused atmosphere at a small women's conference somewhere in California. For sure, these smaller venues can carry a whole lot of the Holy Spirit, and this conference was genuinely powerful. We were worshiping the Lord together, beautifully enclosed within His presence. All I wanted in that moment was to keep basking in His manifest glory, but He had a different plan.

Without warning, His powerful presence came upon my entire person so strongly that I began to shake involuntarily from head to toe. I would not describe the shaking as violent or painful in its intensity, but it was definitely strong and noticeable. Not fully knowing what I was doing, I spoke out in tongues quite loudly, then began to prophesy. The supernatural gifts of

Tongues & interpretation

tongues and interpretation of tongues were in operation. When paired together, they yield a prophetic word. (You can read about this in Acts 10:46 and 19:6 and again in 1 Corinthians 12:7–10.)

I do not remember what I prophesied, but I do remember words that felt like fire spilling out of my mouth. I was fully overcome by the Holy Spirit in that moment, so much so that He could express His passionate heart through me to those in attendance. Looking back, I should have asked more questions about what took place. It was such a new experience for me that I did not even know what questions to ask.

Some months later, at a large midweek service for just youth and young adults, it happened again. Only this time I remember some of what I said, more like what I sang. I recall being comfortably settled toward the back of the meeting hall with some newer friends and chatting before the service started. Soon a highly energetic worship team began to lead everyone in song. They were contagious and passionate with their raw and edgy lyrics, electric guitars and cracking drums. You could not help but to stand to your feet and shout, whistle, clap or jump up and down while they sang out.

As the music became slower and more intimate, I closed my eyes, held my arms up high and outstretched, and felt as if I were swimming in His presence-filled river. There was a sovereign hush that came over the room, and I believe it was a signal that the Holy Spirit was going to speak through someone. Much like before, only without any physical shaking, the Spirit of glory moved upon me this time to sing, not speak, a prophetic message.[1] Without any forethought or forewarning, the heavenly song released out of my mouth with a resonance that seemed to fill the room. Here is the only part of the song that I remember:

> "I have given you My power.
> I have given it this very hour.

Do not leave without My presence,"
says the Lord.

Right now, this song is just words on the page, but back then there was a tangible grace and power that overshadowed the lyrics—so much so that the felt atmosphere of the meeting place lifted into some kind of crescendo. People began clapping and shouting. One young man bolted to the front of the room to give his life to Christ, while others left their seats to walk toward the front of the room in a genuine, spontaneous response to His presence.

Keep in mind, I had only a very limited understanding of what was taking place. I have also heard and read instruction since to use caution when saying, "Thus says the Lord" in connection to prophecy, as it makes you sound too authoritative. I am not sure how accurate this instruction is. I had never been taught to use that signature in the first place; those words simply came out of my mouth. I also did not prophesy again in a corporate setting with this kind of impact for several more years. Still, I was learning that there is a God who still speaks, and He wants to speak powerfully not only *to* you but *through* you. When He speaks through you, realize that these are not just ordinary words—these are heaven-infused prophetic words.

The Origins of Prophetic Ministry

Prophetic ministry, which began first with the Old Testament prophets, has always been sourced to the supernatural working of the Holy Spirit. "No prophecy of Scripture came about by the prophet's own interpretation of things. For prophecy never had its origin in the human will, but prophets, though human, spoke from God as they were carried along by the Holy Spirit" (2 Peter 1:20–21 NIV). Old Testament prophets were hand selected by God to be His ambassadors and spokespersons to the people by communicating His word to them as they received it from Him. True Old Testament prophets were careful to deliver the message that God gave them and not to speak out their own opinions or on their own authority.

We can see how carefully God made His word known to them, even placing His words in their mouths. For example, God affirmed to Moses, "Now go; I will help you speak and will teach you what to say" (Exodus 4:12 NIV). God then assured him, "I will raise up for them a prophet like you, . . . and I will put my words in his mouth. He will tell them everything I command him" (Deuteronomy 18:18 NIV). The Lord said to Jeremiah, "I have put my words in your mouth" (Jeremiah 1:9 NIV). God commissioned Ezekiel by saying, "You must speak my words to them" (Ezekiel 2:7 NIV). Amos claimed, "This is what the LORD says" (Amos 1:3).[2] And many of the Old Testament prophetic books begin with the words, *The word of the LORD that came to . . .* (Jonah 1:1; Joel 1:1; Micah 1:1; see also Hosea 1:2; Zephaniah 1:1).

At the same time, these powerful and influential Old Testament prophets were held to the strictest of standards. In fact, the people were commanded to reject and purge from their midst any so-called prophet who performed a sign or wonder or accurately predicted the future, but then lead them into the worship of idols (see Deuteronomy 13:2). Furthermore, for those who gave a prophetic word that did not come true, then no other explanation could be given. The only acceptable conclusion was they did not hear the Lord, they had spoken falsely in His name and their punishment was to be death (see 18:20, 22).

Even though the Lord had established highly governmental prophets throughout the Old Testament—meaning men and women called by God to lead and articulate His precepts, directives, warnings, judgments and encouragements on His behalf—we also see His heartfelt desire to speak directly to His people without a middleman. You may recall that in the Garden of Eden, God had enjoyed the beauty of unbroken fellowship and communication with His first man and woman, Adam and Eve—that is, until they sinned against Him. Adam and Eve's decision to eat what God commanded them not to eat unraveled their perfect fellowship and collapsed their communication.

Later, as Moses led the Israelites through the wilderness, the Lord summoned the entire nation of Israel to Mount Sinai so He could speak straightway to them all. Then He appeared to them on the mountain as illuminating fire, along with thick smoke, roaring thunder and streaks of lightning. His glorious presence overwhelmed the Israelites, so much so that they rejected the Lord's invitation for unmediated communication. They turned to Moses and said, "Speak to us yourself and we will listen. But do not have God speak to us or we will die" (Exodus 20:19 NIV).

In Numbers 11:11–15, we see Moses again, but this time he is complaining to God over the burden of shepherding those edgy, ill-natured Israelites. In response, God told Moses to gather seventy elders at the tent of meeting. As they came together, God took of His Spirit already on Moses and transferred it to those elders. This anointing, once conferred, made it possible for the elders to help Moses lead the people just as Moses would. Strangely, two men who were listed among the seventy did not make it to the meeting place but stayed in the camp. When the Holy Spirit came upon the 68 elders at the meeting, the two missing elders also began to prophesy in the camp, signifying the Spirit upon Moses had come upon them also.

Moses' closest assistant, Joshua, was provoked by this and demanded that Moses forbid them. Moses' response was, "Are you zealous for my sake? Oh, that all the LORD's people were prophets and that the LORD would put His Spirit upon them!" (verse 29). On the surface this appears to be the flippant response of a frustrated leader. It was not. His response was a prophetic glimpse of something he saw coming in the distant future. There would come a day when God would spiritually enable His men and women in such a way that they would all prophesy.

Centuries later, the prophet Joel spoke into this even more distinctly. He prophesied that the Spirit of God would be poured out on people in an explosion of continuous prophecy, signs and wonders:

> "And it shall come to pass afterward that I will pour out My Spirit on all flesh; your sons and your daughters shall prophesy, your old men shall dream dreams, your young men shall see visions. And also on My menservants and on My maidservants I will pour out My Spirit in those days. And I will show wonders in the heavens and in the earth: blood and fire and pillars of smoke. The sun shall be turned into darkness, and the moon into blood, before the coming of the great and awesome day of the LORD."
>
> Joel 2:28–31

Here, Joel reveals the dynamic ministry of the future. He foresaw the Holy Spirit pouring Himself out upon ordinary men and women, not just the prophets. As a result, everyone could prophesy. Now fast-forward about five hundred years to the gospels and then to the book of Acts. Jesus spoke candidly to His disciples about His approaching and extremely difficult departure but assured them, saying, "It is to your advantage that I go away; for if I do not go away, the Helper will not come to you; but if I depart, I will send Him to you" (John 16:7). The Helper here is in reference to the Holy Spirit. After Jesus' shocking death and phenomenal resurrection, He spent forty heart-stirring final days with His apostles, teaching them God's kingdom realm and proving He was truly alive. Then He gave them a strict commandment not to leave Jerusalem but to wait for the "Promise of the Father" (Acts 1:4), again referring to the Holy Spirit.

As the group of 120 believers waited in prayerful unison in an Upper Room, the Holy Spirit appeared as the sound of a powerful wind that filled the entire house. Tongues of fire appeared miraculously and then rested on each one individually. With this, they began to proclaim the wonders of God supernaturally in languages they had never learned before, which so happened to be the native languages of the visiting delegates to Jerusalem that day. In Acts 2:5, the Jerusalem crowd, composed of Jews "from every nation under heaven," gathered to the sound of these newly anointed disciples while the apostle Peter seized the opportunity. Peter pointed everyone to this same passage in Joel and declared in so many words, *This is that . . . ,* and then gave an outstanding Gospel message. Believers in Jesus have been prophesying ever since.

What Is a Prophetic Word?

In its simplest form, a prophecy is communication from God, either directly to a person or to a person through another person. Again, He communicates in many different ways, something we will explore throughout this book. What makes an inspired communication a prophecy, rather than just ordinary words, is this:

- It clarifies the heart and mind of God in a situation;
- It reveals what is concealed; or
- It declares the future.

We read this in 1 Corinthians 12:7–10:

> But the manifestation of the Spirit is given to each one for the profit of all: for to one is given the word of wisdom through the Spirit, to another the word of knowledge through the same Spirit, . . . to another the working of miracles, to another prophecy.

27

The word *prophecy* here, and every time except once in the New Testament, is the Greek word *prophēteia*. It means "what is clarified beforehand; prophecy which involves divinely empowered forthtelling (asserting the mind of God) or foretelling (prediction)."[3] To prophesy (*prophéteuó*), then, means to reveal "the mind (message) of God in a particular situation" and may also refer to "predicting the future as the Lord reveals it."[4]

New Testament prophetic words are weighted differently than those in the Old Testament, and they are to be tested for congruency with the existing Scriptures in order to be accepted or not. The biblical canon, referring to our authorized and accepted set of scriptural texts, is now closed, and prophetic words will no longer be added to them in the form of "new revelation."[5] The apostles must have recognized the human element now attached to the gift of prophecy, which stirred Paul to say, "Do not despise prophecies. Test all things; hold fast what is good" (1 Thessalonians 5:20–21).

Here is one practical, real-life example.

Taylor, an art business owner, received a prophetic word in a dream one Saturday night, not knowing she would minister that exact word the very next morning. She dreamt she was walking down a familiar street beside a homeless woman who had suffered much emotional anguish as a result of several abusive relationships. In the dream, when Taylor confided to her, "I have a word from God for you," the woman stared straight at her in unbelief, laughed, then asked, "What do you have to say?" Taylor responded, "Don't throw your pearls to pigs" (quoting Matthew 7:6 NLT). At this statement, the woman began to weep and the dream ended.

The next morning, Taylor and her husband arrived early to church. While her husband prepared the technical requirements for the morning services, Taylor waited outside in her car, quietly journaling the dream from the night before. She looked out her window and noticed three homeless women sitting nearby on a grassy area in front of the church building. Because Taylor knew one of them, she stepped out of her car excitedly and said, "Good morning!"

At her greeting, one of the other women began to share her story with Taylor. She described her marriage and separation from a violent and abusive husband who had physically threatened her for having a relationship with Jesus, among other things. She had also lost her job and housing just four days before. Sensing this was the woman in the dream, Taylor listened empathetically, then gave her the prophetic word. "God spoke to me about you in a dream last night. He told me to tell you, 'Don't throw your pearls to pigs!'" At this, the woman began to weep because her middle name was Pearl. Without question, she knew God was speaking to her about her future.

Along those lines, Judy, a paralegal and one of many outstanding prayer ministers at Harvest Church in Turlock, California, shared a unique story with me. She said, "When I walked into my hair appointment, the Holy Spirit told me my hairdresser was pregnant." As Judy and her hairdresser conversed back and forth, Judy brought up the subject of children and asked if she and her husband planned on having them. Her hairdresser confided how they had tried to conceive for five years unsuccessfully after numerous doctor appointments and tests. What Judy said next came as quite a shock. "The Holy Spirit says you are pregnant right now!" Three weeks after their conversation, Judy received a phone call. Her hairdresser called to confirm the good news that she was indeed pregnant.

Perhaps you have heard instruction before concerning this kind of prophetic word, namely never to prophesy someone's pregnancy. There are good reasons for this, as some have prophesied someone's desperate desire, only it was not the word of the Lord. In so doing, they were hurtful and not helpful, because they gave false hope. Regardless, should the mistakes of others determine what we say or do not say when we have truly discerned the prophetic word of the Lord?

Absolutely not. I would rather we keep pressing in for accuracy in the prophetic rather than backing off because others have missed it. If you do prophesy something that does not come true, thankfully you are no longer subject to the death penalty. The only thing now subject to death is just your pride. Still, if you do not develop prophetic accuracy or take responsibility for your mistakes, you will lose your credibility.

To prophesy in truth, we would first need to be given the supernatural ability to do so from the Holy Spirit. There are different ways to receive this gift, too. You can ask the Holy Spirit for it yourself, or you can have someone with this gift lay their hands on you to receive it.[6]

The apostle Paul exhorted us to "pursue love, and desire spiritual gifts, but especially that you may prophesy" (1 Corinthians 14:1). When he said to desire spiritual gifts, the specific gifts most often referred to in chapter 12 are words of wisdom, words of knowledge, the gift of faith, "gifts of healings," the working of miracles, prophecy, discerning of spirits, tongues and the interpretation of tongues (verses 7–10).

Some people entertain the false belief that they are being prideful or self-serving for wanting such supernatural abilities in the first place. Pursuing the gifts of the Holy Spirit, however, especially the anointing to prophesy, means you are pursuing the heart of God toward others. These powerful manifestations of the Spirit serve as God's kiss and embrace to those who are hopeless, those who are estranged from God and those who have little to no knowledge of God at all.

Kingdom Principles

1. Prophetic ministry first began with the Old Testament prophets and has always been sourced to the supernatural working of the Holy Spirit.

2. Even though the Lord had established highly governmental prophets throughout the Old Testament to speak on His behalf, we also see His heartfelt desire to speak directly to His people without a middleman.

3. Both Moses and Joel foresaw the ministry of the distant future, namely that all would prophesy.

4. New Testament prophetic words are weighted differently than those in the Old Testament. They are no longer being added to the biblical canon as "new revelation."

5. To prophesy in truth, we would first need to be given the supernatural ability to do so from the Holy Spirit.

Thoughts for Reflection

1. Have you ever prophesied before? What were the results?

2. How is prophecy for us today just as much as it was in the Old Testament? What are some differences?

3. How is it possible for every Christian to prophesy?

4. Have you ever heard a prophetic word that seemed lifeless or, perhaps, even pointless? If it is a supernatural gift, why would this happen?

5. Do you feel it is prideful or arrogant to pursue the Holy Spirit's gift of prophecy or other supernatural gifts? Has this chapter helped you to reconcile those feelings?

Prophetic Words Need
Prophetic Wisdom

While making a purchase at a popular retail store, I experienced an all-too-familiar feeling when I observed the many purchasers standing in line ahead of me. I say this somewhat humorously, but I have a certain dread of standing in these long checkout lines—so much so that I have abandoned many such lines before, including my intended purchases, because I did not have the patience to wait. On this occasion, there were six or seven customers waiting in front of me, coupled with the usual shortage of available cashiers. Normally this was enough cause for me to exit. Only I did not make an exit because something unexpected began to happen to me spiritually.

I felt my eyes fix upon a young mother making her purchases at the head of the line. When I say that my eyes fixed upon her, I mean one of those Holy Spirit–inspired laser-beam stares, like the one we read of in Acts 3:4 when Peter's eyes became fixed on the lame beggar right before he carried out a miraculous healing by the unction of the Holy Spirit. This supernatural phenomenon is often a prophetic pointer toward something the Holy Spirit is about to do. Thankfully, she was turned away from me and did not notice my stare, or that would have been too uncomfortable.

It took a few moments, but I realized that I recognized her. Alisa (not her real name) attended my church on occasion, and I knew her mother quite well. I noticed how she was holding an active toddler with her one hand and then a baby on her hip. I also noted that her hair had been cut short, the kind of short hairstyle that busy mothers choose to save time. As real as all of this looked, I knew by the Holy Spirit that it was not real. In this unusual prophetic vision, I was not seeing this woman in the here and now; I was seeing her in her future. In reality, she did not have two children. She had only one, and her hair was not short either. It was down to her waist. What was going on?

The next day I sent a text message to her mother, asking, "Is your daughter, Alisa, pregnant?" She replied, "Not that I know of. Why?" I explained the unusual vision and then prophesied to her that another grandchild was coming. She was a fiery intercessor and received my vision as coming from the Holy Spirit. Then I communicated the miscellaneous detail about her daughter's hairstyle since it seemed to stand out so clearly.

Around three months later, her mother contacted me with much enthusiasm. "Alisa is pregnant!" she exclaimed. We had a joyful exchange over their good news, and I congratulated her on the new grandbaby to come. Within just days of our conversation, however, there occurred an alarming circumstance when her daughter began to bleed heavily as if she were having a miscarriage. "I was so tempted to be afraid and agree with death," Alisa later explained. "I had miscarried my previous pregnancy, and it appeared to be happening all over again."

Hospital technicians searched for, but could not find, the baby's heartbeat and then informed her that she was probably losing the pregnancy. Her mother, being a woman of faith, reminded Alisa of the prophetic vision. Because of the prophetic word, she prayed very confidently and assured her, "Everything will be okay." Miraculously, her daughter and the baby overcame this first hurdle. Alisa kept the pregnancy, her blood test numbers remained strong and finally the technicians rediscovered the baby's heartbeat.

Six months into the pregnancy, some new concerns emerged—the baby was measuring too small and possibly not growing properly. Then at seven months, Alisa was also diagnosed with gestational diabetes. Both mother and daughter continued to hold on to the prophetic vision, and Alisa communicated a strong feeling of internal peace about the outcome of the pregnancy. Just as the Holy Spirit revealed, her baby boy was born in perfect health and at the right size. I should also add here that Alisa did cut her hair to her shoulders not too long after her son's birth.

Surprisingly, the biggest problem was not the health of the baby during and after the pregnancy, even though there were obvious difficulties. Alisa's bigger problem was with her husband. She went on to disclose that she was in a turbulent marriage to a violent and unpredictable man. "He was connected to criminals and dealing drugs, among other things," she said. "When he was arrested and jailed for a violent kidnapping, I filed for divorce." To further add to her grief, her mother became very ill and died right around the same time.

"God knew all of this was coming to me," Alisa explained. "If I had lost the baby in addition to my mother and my husband, it would have been too much." Then she expressed, "Most people can only handle so much loss before they completely lose their ability to cope." After describing her son, in addition to her fabulous daughter, as being an absolute and unending joy to her life, she ended our conversation on a very upbeat and confident note, saying, "My son's life is living proof of God's goodness, and I am at peace."

I introduced this chapter with the true story of Alisa and her mother to show you the gift of prophecy in action and then what happens when you join a prophetic word with something called prophetic wisdom, a concept I will begin to explain next. To understand what prophetic wisdom is, we first need to define *prophetic* and *wisdom* separately, but then bring them back together to display their powerful partnership. The next section will touch on these two words briefly, but I will illustrate both of them much more thoroughly throughout the book.

Waging Warfare with Prophetic Words

Alisa's journey began when she received a prophetic word from the Holy Spirit through me. A prophetic word is a type of revelatory communication from the Holy Spirit—either directly to a person, or to a person through another person—that reveals what is concealed or declares the future. A prophetic word will emerge supernaturally when the gift of prophecy is in operation, and this gift is one of the nine supernatural gifts of the Holy Spirit that we see listed in 1 Corinthians 12:7–10.

Keep in mind that the Holy Spirit likes to speak in many different ways[1] and might communicate a prophetic word through a vision, a dream, in the form of phrases or words to your heart or in some other interesting way. We are strongly encouraged to desire spiritual gifts, but especially the ability to prophesy.[2] Paul's exhortation to desire the gift of prophecy more than the other supernatural gifts infers the high value that heaven places on genuine prophetic words. A prophetic word, then, is not the mere wish or desire conjured from the heart of another human being. It is a word that flows from the treasury of God's own heart, a word that becomes a bridge between heaven and earth with the supernatural power to create into our natural realm whatever He has spoken.

With that in mind, have you ever received a prophetic word that you knew without a doubt was from God? And then after you received it, did the opposite happen instead? Or nothing at all? The apostle Paul provides us with clear, firm instruction: "This charge I commit to you, son Timothy, according to the prophecies previously made concerning you, that by them you may wage the good warfare" (1 Timothy 1:18). Notice how he connected Timothy's ability to wage a good warfare through the effective use of his prophecies.

Apparently, you can have a prophetic word—a crystal-clear communication from the Holy Spirit about something in the future—but still lose what God intended for you to gain if you do not make use of your prophecies. This reveals our intimate partnership with the Holy Spirit. He releases a prophetic word to you, but our response to the prophecy will often determine the final outcome. This is why we need prophetic wisdom. Prophetic wisdom will escort us through the process that accompanies a prophetic word. And this kind of wisdom is clearly not from human origin, but a supernatural wisdom that comes from the Holy Spirit.

When Abram received a prophetic word from God about his future, that his numerous descendants would possess an inheritance of land that God was leading them to, he needed prophetic wisdom to guide him through. What God promised seemed impossible. He and his wife, Sarai, being 75 and 65 years respectively, were told they would have a child. God assured him in this manner, "Then He brought him outside and said, 'Look now toward heaven, and count the stars if you are able to number them.' And He said to him, 'So shall your descendants be'" (Genesis 15:5). Yet ten years passed and they still had not conceived a child.

Sarai then took control and created her own solution. "So Sarai said to Abram, 'See now, the LORD has restrained me from bearing children. Please, go in to my maid; perhaps I shall obtain children by her.' And Abram heeded the voice of Sarai" (16:2). After she gave her maid, Hagar, to Abram, Hagar conceived a son and named him Ishmael. This was not prophetic wisdom, however. This was human wisdom, and human wisdom comes with consequences.

When it was time for the prophetic word to come to pass, God clarified that Abram and Sarai would, without a surrogate, have a child of destiny together (see 18:10). And to prove His point, He renamed them from Abram and Sarai, father and mother of a multitude, to Abraham and Sarah, father and mother of nations (see 17:5, 15). Everything God spoke to Abraham and Sarah happened. Together they brought forth their son Isaac at the shocking ages of one hundred and ninety, respectively.

The consequences of human wisdom emerged when Ishmael treated his younger brother, Isaac, with contempt and was forced out of the home by Sarah along with his mother, Hagar (see 21:9–10). Interestingly, there are many who suggest Ishmael's descendants (most likely Arabs and other Middle Easterners) have continued that original contempt over the centuries and to this day toward Isaac's descendants, the Israelites, although some dispute this genealogy and claim.[3] The story of Abraham and Sarah illustrates how a clear prophetic word from God about the future still needs to be shaped and finished off with prophetic wisdom.

The impactful partnership between the prophetic and supernatural wisdom was present at creation. In Genesis 1, God created the heavens and the earth through the spoken word: "Let there be light" (verse 3), "Let the earth abound with herbs, grass, and fruit trees" (verse 11) and "Let the waters abound with an abundance of living creatures" (verse 20). As He spoke out these different things, an earth that was without form and void began to take shape in accordance with His words.

Next, we see wisdom in personified form working side by side with Him as He created. The embodied wisdom describes herself[4] here in Proverbs 8:22–30:

> "The LORD possessed me at the beginning of His way, before His works of old. I have been established from everlasting, from the beginning, before there was ever an earth. When there were no depths I was brought forth, when there were no fountains abounding with water. Before the mountains were settled, before the hills, I was brought forth; while as yet He had not made the earth or the fields, or the primal dust of the world. When He prepared the heavens, I was there, when He drew a circle on the face of the deep, when He established the clouds above, when He strengthened the fountains of the deep, when He assigned to the sea its limit, so that the waters would not transgress His command, when He marked out the foundations of the earth, then I was beside Him as a master craftsman; and I was daily His delight, rejoicing always before Him."

Perhaps this expands your paradigm about wisdom. When you think of wisdom in general, what thought or picture comes to mind? Do you envision an older sage (man or woman) who can speak guidance to you from their rich well of life experience? One online dictionary describes this kind of wisdom as "the quality of having experience, knowledge, and good judgement."[5] Knowledge combined with experience does produce a form of wisdom that puts order into our lives so we can live well. The Bible provides us a wealth of such wisdom, especially in the books of Job, Psalms, Proverbs, Ecclesiastes and James.

At the same time, God's wisdom is multifaceted. There are aspects of wisdom that carry such deep spiritual dimensions that we will never see it or lay hold of it unless the Holy Spirit reveals it to us. So in one sense, wisdom acts as a divinely undergirded way of thinking and acting that provides an orderly life. In another sense, wisdom presents itself much like the gift of prophecy in that it has to be unveiled to us by the Spirit and then unpacked prayerfully. I believe this is why the apostle Paul prayed for the Ephesians to have "the spirit of wisdom and revelation in the knowledge of Him" (Ephesians 1:17).

According to Rick Renner, a respected Bible teacher and pastor of the Moscow Good News Church, the English word *wisdom* in Ephesians 1:17 comes from *sophia*,[6] "an old Greek word that was used to describe *insight* or *wisdom not naturally attained*. In other words, this is not natural human wisdom—this is *special insight*."[7] And the word *revelation* comes from the Greek word *apokalupsis*,[8] referring to "something that has been veiled or hidden for a long time and then suddenly, almost instantaneously, becomes clear and visible to the mind or eye."[9] Basically, operating in the prophetic allows the curtains to be pulled back, allowing us to see something that was previously hidden. We can surmise that prophetic wisdom is wisdom that is hidden from us until God chooses to reveal it, since it is past our ordinary understanding.

The good thing is, God promised to give us His wisdom. "If any of you lacks wisdom, let him ask of God, who gives to all liberally and without reproach, and it will be given to him" (James 1:5). God does not withhold His wisdom from us, but He does stipulate that we need to ask Him for it. Now armed with this understanding, when we receive a genuine prophetic word, we should ask for prophetic wisdom, too. Still, this prayer might not ever cross our lips if we allow Satan to steal our prophetic words from us. I will explain how this can happen.

Satan Tries to Steal the Word

International evangelist Mario Murillo is a crusade-style evangelist who moves in the Holy Spirit's gifts of the word of knowledge for supernatural healing and creative miracles. His preaching ministry was birthed in the "drug-obsessed, violent, and occult-saturated student revolution of Berkeley, California," where he "saw thousands of young students give their lives to Christ."[10] Mario continues his aggressive ministry aimed at the most violent and overlooked youth of America while challenging the lukewarm, passive Church to become contagiously fervent with the Holy Spirit once again.[11]

While ministering at one of our campuses, Harvest Church in downtown Turlock, California, Mario shared with the crowd a time when he was rebuked by the Holy Spirit.[12] He explained that he was in prayer when he heard the Holy Spirit say, *You've been robbed, and you're okay with it.* Shocked, Mario shot back, *How have I been robbed?* The Holy Spirit clarified that two million dollars had been stolen from him. Mario illustrated how this happened with the story of a multimillionaire who had been prompted by the Lord to give him a million dollars. The problem was, he wanted Mario to use the money to start and pastor a church. Mario explained that he was an evangelist, not a pastor, and asked, "Why can't you just give it for souls?" The millionaire insisted that the money be for a church in this man's preferred city. (Mario expressed his thoughts to us, saying, "How wicked is it when God prospers you, and you put strings on your offering?") So Mario replied, "'I'm gonna call my friend, 'cause he's always wanted to plant a church in your city," then had the funds transferred to his friend, who built a work there and assigned someone to pastor the church. After the church was built, the new pastor promised to give Mario an acre of land as a gift. But three months later, he called Mario again and said they were not going to give him the land after all. Mario brought it all together after he explained the Holy Spirit's clear prophetic word to him. The Spirit had already told him, *You will have two million dollars for your ministry. It's comin'.*

A few years later, Mario was ministering in Adelaide, Australia, at a large convention of seven thousand people. Outside the convention center was a backslidden twentysomething man who came into the meeting to meet girls, not God. Out of all the people, Mario was prompted to invite him to stand up. He stood up, and Mario prophesied by the Spirit, "When you walk to your car at the end of this meeting and you put your key in the door, you will receive an invention that will make you wealthy beyond your wildest dreams." Just like that, after the meeting the young man walked to his car, put the key in the door and was given the supernatural understanding to create a medical invention by the Holy Spirit. Consider that he had no background in medicine or chemistry, but all of a sudden he had supernatural insight. He spent the next four years patenting this invention while the pharmaceutical companies declared a very real war on him because they saw its potential. His case went all the way to the Australian Supreme Court, which awarded him millions of dollars. Much later, he asked to meet Mario for lunch to say thank you for the word he had been given. Mario thought, *I'm gettin' two million dollars today!* The young man kept thanking him but only paid for the meal and left.

After several more stories like this, Mario came to the punch line. "God's words are now to be enforced! His promises to us are to be enforced!"[13] His point was, if you do not enforce the word, you will lose it. It will be stolen. This was the reason the Holy Spirit rebuked him. He rebuked him for his unbelief, because unbelief is passive with prophetic words and Mario had not prayed into, sought wisdom for or done anything to lay hold of that promise.

Your prophetic words are powerful, effective weapons, but *only when you use them.* When you do not, you give Satan grounds to steal your prophetic words from you.

You Will Overcome with Prophetic Wisdom

In the Bible, Jesus often taught the crowds using parables— earthly stories that have a heavenly meaning.[14] For example, the Parable of the Sower, which on the surface appears to be a lesson about agriculture, is really a spiritual teaching about the condition of the heart and how to receive God's revealed Word. In Mark 4:3–8, Jesus spoke to the crowd, saying this:

> "Listen! Behold, a sower went out to sow. And it happened, as he sowed, that some seed fell by the wayside; and the birds of the air came and devoured it. Some fell on stony ground, where it did not have much earth; and immediately it sprang up because it had no depth of earth. But when the sun was up it was scorched, and because it had no root it withered away. And some seed fell among thorns; and the thorns grew up and choked it, and it yielded no crop. But other seed fell on good ground and yielded a crop that sprang up, increased and produced: some thirtyfold, some sixty, and some a hundred."

Later, Jesus revealed the deeper meaning of this parable to His disciples. The seed sown represents the Word of God, thus implying that the Word acts like a seed that grows something when planted. He also described four conditions of the heart, again inferring that the heart is like soil to be planted in, and the way people receive God's Word as either wayside, stony, thorny or good: Wayside people have a hard heart, making the Word an easy steal by Satan because the seed never got planted in the first place. For stony-ground people, the Word seems exciting at first, yet cannot take root when planted in the shallow soil of their hearts. The distractions and worries in the hearts of thorny-ground people create crowded conditions for the Word; the seed takes root and grows, but there is not enough room for it to thrive and produce anything. Finally, good-ground people receive the Word unhindered into their hearts. Not only does the Word get firmly planted, but it grows and reproduces visibly in their lives.

Jesus taught us how to receive God's Word, whether from the pages of His Bible, through a Sunday sermon or for the purposes of this book, through a prophetic word either from the Holy Spirit to our own heart or from the lips of another person. The condition of our heart determines how well we will receive that prophetic word. And then prophetic wisdom is our *ability to respond properly to the prophetic word and partner with the Holy Spirit for His divinely intended outcome.* If we have a hard heart, which is an unbelieving heart, a genuine prophetic word from God becomes "steal-able" by Satan himself. Satan only steals what is of value, and he is after these prophetic words to stop them from reproducing and to hinder God's kingdom from advancing in us and through us.

Alisa and her mother understood this principle and were able to wage "good warfare" for the life of her unborn baby. When presented with another potential outcome, namely death and possible deformity, they received prophetic wisdom from the Holy Spirit and knew how to respond. Their inspired instructions came from Scripture, specifically Proverbs 18:21, which teaches that "death and life are in the power of the tongue, and those who love it will eat its fruit," and Mark 11:23: "For assuredly, I say to you, whoever says to this mountain, 'Be removed and be cast into the sea,' and does not doubt in his heart, but believes that those things he says will be done, he will have whatever he says." Mother and grandmother united in faith over the prophetic word, believing that death and deformity were lies from the devil himself and that life and healing were the absolute truth. And they proclaimed this truth, not the lies, in faith before the Lord, to their enemy, the devil, and to each other without backing down. They knew this was not a natural battle but a spiritual one, and one that required spiritual weapons to overcome.

Does it still surprise you, then, that a prophetic word does not just happen? That it needs our partnership conjoined with prophetic wisdom to come to pass?

Take for example the prophet Daniel, who took notice of the prophetic time frame given by the prophet Jeremiah for the release of his people from Babylonian exile (see Daniel 9; Jeremiah 29:10). According to Jeremiah's prophecy, freedom was at hand. The new Persian ruler, King Cyrus, had released the Jews to go back to Jerusalem, yet many chose not to go or were hindered from doing what they set out to do. Daniel needed more understanding of this and turned back to God with prayer, fasting and mourning. After 21 days of consecration, an angel appeared to him and told him an unusual story. The angel shared that he was dispatched to Daniel from heaven on the first day Daniel prayed, but a demonic spirit assigned to the land of Persia had stopped the angel from advancing to reach Daniel. Finally, the archangel Michael came and fought against the demonic prince of Persia. As a result, Daniel's messenger angel broke through and appeared to Daniel with some real answers about what awaited his people (see Daniel 10:1–21).[15] Daniel was not passive about the prophetic word. Instead, he pressed in to Jeremiah's prophecy with prayer and fasting until the angel came and gave him prophetic wisdom.

Too often, people have a prophetic promise, but they lack a wise application. For example, someone wrote to me and said something like this: "I had a vision where I saw myself in front of Jesus with two angels by my side, and I wore a coat of many colors. Later I heard the Holy Spirit in a dream say, *You will minister to kings and rulers.* What does this mean?" What an incredible calling to receive through a vision and a dream. Unfortunately, this person had no clue what it meant, let alone how to respond. And when people lack prophetic wisdom, the word will most likely not come to pass. Or even worse circumstances might occur, and they are left wandering, waiting and wondering as to why. On the other hand, when you have the prophetic word and join it with prophetic wisdom, your ordinary life will become an extraordinary one. Trouble will come, but through prophetic wisdom you will always overcome and have a good testimony.

Kingdom Principles

1. A prophetic word is a type of revelatory communication from the Holy Spirit—either directly to a person, or to a person through another person—that reveals what is concealed or declares the future.
2. You can have a prophetic word—a crystal-clear communication from the Holy Spirit about something in the future—but still lose what God intended for you to gain, if you do not make use of your prophecies.
3. When we receive a genuine prophetic word, we should ask the Holy Spirit for prophetic wisdom too.
4. To understand what prophetic wisdom is, we first need to define *prophetic* and *wisdom* separately, but then bring them back together to display their powerful partnership.
5. Prophetic wisdom will escort us through the process that accompanies a prophetic word. And this kind of wisdom is clearly not from human origin, but a wisdom that comes from the Holy Spirit.

Thoughts for Reflection

1. Have you ever had a clear prophetic word from God, only it did not come to pass? After reading this chapter, do you know why this happened?
2. Have you ever successfully waged "the good warfare" (1 Timothy 1:18) with your prophetic words?
3. Satan can steal our prophetic words if we have a hard and unbelieving heart. How would you know if you have that kind of heart?

4. Have you ever considered the partnership between a prophetic word and prophetic wisdom? How could you become more intentional in making this connection?

5. Have you ever tried to make a prophetic word from God come to pass on your terms using human wisdom? What did you learn from that experience?

Perceiving the Prophetic Word

I was still a very new Christian and a new congregant to this Pentecostal-style Foursquare church in Modesto, California. The senior pastor was fairly young himself, around thirty years old, and his Sunday morning sermon was heartfelt and authentic. Although I do not remember his exact words, I recall the passion in his voice as he spoke out on the flawless integrity of God, quoting Numbers 23:19: "God is not like people, who lie. . . . Whatever he promises, he does; he speaks, and it is done" (GNT).

It sounds ridiculous now, but my self-talk during his sermon was off the chain. Is it just me, or do we all have a rebellious inner voice that can sound off so powerfully at times that you have to hold your face in check? As he spoke, my inner voice began saying something like, *Hmmm. Really? Did you just say that God never lies?* Then the dialogue continued with a string of more arguments, again all on the inside of me. *That's so not true. Everyone lies. I'm sure God lies. I mean, He has to have—*

Right about there, I was interrupted by a strong voice with deep undertones that was not my own internal response. The voice, which I would describe more as a muffled boom, projected just one powerful truth: *Does God really lie?* Not only did the Spirit of the Lord rebuke and convict my heart, but I was very grateful I had perceived the voice of God. He loved me so much that He reached right in and set the record straight, which is why I esteem God's rebukes as beautiful.

This was not my first supernatural experience with His life-altering voice. Months before and just moments before yielding my broken life to Jesus, I had an encounter with His voice—not an audible voice, but the perceptible awareness of His heart and powerful presence that contained one distinct message: *I accept you as you are.*

His voice ministered deeply to my fractured soul steeped in LDS teachings, all of which were performance driven and impossible. I had consistently failed their high standards and never felt good enough. He spoke straightway into my deficit, and in turn I surrendered my life to Him.

What I realized only later was that He was strategically preparing me to learn His voice from the very beginning—and not only to perceive His voice, but in time and at His leading to reveal and give voice to His prophetic secrets as I discerned them.

Perceiving the Holy Spirit's prophetic word begins with first perceiving His voice. Did you notice that initially He did not speak to me with enunciated sentence clarity? Have you, too, ever experienced His voice in perhaps the same or a different way?

While it is true that He does speak plainly at times, His voice can also come as a feeling, an internal sound, an identifiable thought and a whole lot more. Perceiving His voice, then, is not about how clearly or loudly He speaks to you, but more about your heart having been prepared to perceive.

Children Perceive More Easily

Minister and author Madeline James can remember the first time she heard the voice of God. Madeline's parents had made an intentional decision as a family to serve the Lord wholeheartedly and break every generational curse in the process. "We went to church several times a week as a result," Madeline explained. God honored her parents' unwavering commitment to Him, and during an altar call while at children's church, Madeline, as a five-year-old, heard His voice with perfect clarity. He said, *I want to come and live inside your heart. Will you let Me in?*

Madeline can remember the incident as if it were yesterday. In response to His clear voice, she looked up to heaven and invited Jesus to come live inside her heart. In doing so, she felt His deep, love-filled presence enfold her in such a way that her deep struggles with separation anxiety and unexplained fear began to heal. This encounter also conditioned her to be sensitive and hungry for the voice of God, a posture that positioned her for highly visible prophetic ministry as an adult.

Have you noticed that children often hear or see the voice of the Lord with greater clarity than adults do? We read these words of Jesus in Matthew 5:8: "Blessed are the pure in heart, for they shall see God." Children are very pure hearted. They have not yet learned to filter out His voice through unbelief, logic and reason—or through the lens of life's disappointments.

At our church, and for this reason, we equip and activate children, much like we do with adults, in how to distinguish God's voice and then prophesy at His leading. When you tell children that the Holy Spirit is going to speak to them, that He is a communicator and will tell them something about a person if they ask Him to, almost instantly they receive a phrase or picture in their hearts from Him. Here are a few examples:

- A child who attended one of our kid's clubs at an elementary school campus prophesied to another child during their weekly club gathering. She said specifically, "You are getting a new home, and your mom will have another baby!" The school year soon ended, and these two children did not see each other again until after the summer break. When they reunited the following school year, again at the kid's club, the child who was prophesied to confirmed that they did get a new home over the summer and his mother was again pregnant.

• Another child had refused to participate during a time of worship and prayer at our regular Sunday children's service. He was angry at God that day because he had a disease and had not been healed yet. While the other kids worshiped exuberantly in song, he experienced an open vision and saw Jesus in heaven. (An open vision can also be referred to as a trance, which is a biblical experience in which you seem to lose contact with your natural surroundings and enter into another reality by the power of the Holy Spirit.[1]) In the vision Jesus asked him, "What do you want to see around here?" The boy said, "I want to see where You hang out." Jesus then escorted him to His throne room and showed him around. Later the boy described where Jesus sat, referring to His throne in the throne room, and the many rainbows that were "around His chair."[2] What made this young boy's vision even more exciting was the Bible lesson already planned out for that day, something he did not have any foreknowledge of, was a lesson about the throne room of God.

Children perceive the voice of the Spirit with refreshing accuracy largely due to their unfiltered and guileless hearts. As childhood turns to adulthood, however, negative beliefs and inferior attitudes set in and cloud our ability to distinguish God's voice accurately.

In 1 Corinthians 13:9 we read: "For we know in part and we prophesy in part." Have you noticed that God speaks most often in headlines, sound bites and quick glimpses? He does not give us the whole picture, which is mostly about our darkened ability to perceive His voice in fullness in the first place, something I believe the Holy Spirit wants to remedy.

Any belief that holds us more strongly than the truth of His written Word will bend and distort His voice accordingly when it comes.

> "Therefore speak to them, and say to them, 'Thus says the LORD God: "Every one of the house of Israel who sets up his idols in his heart, and puts before him what causes him to stumble into iniquity, and then comes to the prophet, I the LORD will answer him who comes, according to the multitude of his idols."'"
>
> Ezekiel 14:4

What does it mean that God will answer an Israelite "according to the multitude of his idols"?[3] When Ezekiel made reference to idols, he was referring to the vile practices of worshiping other gods in addition to worshiping Yahweh. We can envision the wayward Israelite going off somewhere, perhaps to a shrine they have built at home or to a designated temple nearby, and then performing some kind of prayer, offering or ritual to a false god. No matter where they paid homage to a physical idol, this verse made it clear that the idol ruled them from the altar of their own hearts. As a result, anything that God chose to say to them became shaded, influenced and voiced over by the idol as a result.

Most Christians would not dare worship another god in this manner. Still, we often have heart issues that can shade and twist the pure voice of God when He speaks—habitual sin, unbelief, disappointments, selfish agendas or rebellion, just to name a few. After King David committed adultery with Bathsheba and attempted to cover it up by having her husband killed, he realized the source of his problem to be his own sick heart. Then he prayed a desperate prayer: "Create in me a clean heart, O God; and renew a right spirit within me" (Psalm 51:10 KJV). We all have a tendency to close our hearts to His voice when He says something hard to hear.

The writer of Hebrews issued a powerful warning in this regard: "Today, if you will hear His voice, do not harden your hearts as in the rebellion" (3:15). A heart that can perceive the voice of God accurately is a purified and tender heart. With the leading of the Holy Spirit, we can step into a renewing of our heart beginning with one simple prayer: *Create in me a clean heart, O God!* It is a daily process, but submitting our hearts in this manner is something He delights in. As you allow Him to transform your thoughts, biases and emotions, you will perceive His wonderful voice with increasing clarity.

I had mentioned my maturing moment while listening to the preaching of the young pastor in the beginning of this chapter. That same year, he and his wife had invited me to participate in their newly launched children's ministry program, believing the Holy Spirit had directed them to do so. "This is the will of God," he said. "God wants you to do this." I had no desire to be involved in children's ministry and thought it was an odd conversation at best, so I declined their invitation, and for other reasons I left his church to join a much larger Pentecostal church in the same city, a church I really enjoyed and grew in. Surprisingly, the children's pastor at this church approached me in a similar manner, saying, "God told me to talk to you about children's ministry." I declined again, because I knew I was not called to children's ministry.

Five or six years later, once I had graduated from college and gotten married, my husband was the newly appointed associate pastor for our present church, Bethel Temple in Turlock, California (now called Harvest Church). When the volunteer children's pastor resigned her duties all of a sudden, we stepped in, thinking it would be for the short term, but after more than a year, my husband was being referred to as the "children's pastor." He was great at it, but we were not called to children's ministry and considered going to another church as a result. The good news is, finally a children's pastor was found, allowing my husband to move back into his original role as the associate pastor.

Why then would people prophesy and agree with a spiritual direction over our life that was inconsistent with the clear direction inside our own heart? At best, it was done in ignorance. At worst, it was prophetic manipulation. Personal agendas, biases and preferences can sound like the voice of God inside of us if we do not continuously submit our heart motives to the Holy Spirit and to the washing of the written Word.

Become Sensitive to the Written Word

The first Bible I received as a new Christian was a New Testament in a modern, conversational translation known as *The Message*. This version of the Bible is not a literal Greek translation, but a modern paraphrase, and I devoured it from beginning to end, totally thrilled that it used language I could relate to. Up until then, I had read just the King James translation since it was the only LDS-approved version of the Bible, but I found it difficult to understand. During those first few years as a Christian, however, I spent several hours a day reading the more contemporary, popular translations, which left me wanting to read more.

My hunger for the written Word was so strong that I kept imagining myself tearing pages out of my Bible and physically eating them. This was just my extraordinary imagination, of course, but my insatiable appetite drove me into several months of persistent study. The benefits were many, but in particular was the growing perception of His voice speaking to my heart. I could distinguish it because the nature and content of His communication would match up with something I had read in the Bible.

For example, I could identify His felt peace on the decisions I was considering for my life, decisions not easily accepted by my immediate family. I had read in the Bible that He is the "Prince of Peace" (Isaiah 9:6) and that we are to allow His peace to rule our hearts (see Colossians 3:15). His felt peace, then, was actually His voice endorsing my life choices. No, He did not enunciate this in a clear statement to my heart; instead, He sounded off with His emotions, something I could now distinguish thanks to studying His Word.

The written Word sifts and washes our inner thoughts and intentions, the very stuff that colors over His pure voice or blocks it out altogether. We read in Hebrews, "For the word of God is living and powerful, and sharper than any two-edged sword, piercing even to the division of soul and spirit, and of joints and marrow, and is a discerner of the thoughts and intents of the heart" (4:12). Sometimes the sifting happens immediately upon encountering a Bible passage that applies to your present circumstances.

Lorri from Texas, for example, shared about her former friendship with a group of Christian women whom she described as "gossipy, strifeful, and slandering." She did not realize that their negative attitudes were impacting her as much as they were, and after a season of interaction she, too, began to carry the same spirit and gossip about others just as much. During this same time frame, Lorri began attending an in-depth study of the book of Isaiah, during which she came across this eye-opening passage:

> So I said: "Woe is me, for I am undone! Because I am a man of unclean lips, and I dwell in the midst of a people of unclean lips; for my eyes have seen the King, the LORD of hosts."

Then one of the seraphim flew to me, having in his hand a live coal which he had taken with the tongs from the altar. And he touched my mouth with it, and said: "Behold, this has touched your lips; your iniquity is taken away, and your sin purged."

Isaiah 6:5–7

Lorri felt the undeniable conviction of the Holy Spirit as she read this passage. In response, she repented sincerely from her heart for engaging in the "sin of the tongue," asking the Lord to cleanse her lips "with coal." Then, realizing the ungodly and negative impact they had on her, she backed away from this group. "From that point on," she shared, "I committed to having a pure heart and to only speak well of others." As a result, Lorri has not only grown in character and maturity, but she has also grown in prophetic ministry and accuracy.

When God trusts you with people, He entrusts you with more information about people. Maturing prophetic voices have learned to not say everything God reveals to them. Instead, they seek prophetic wisdom on what to say and what not to say and then act accordingly. Other times, the sifting process happens more indirectly. You have put the Word in your heart, but then circumstances occur much later, causing that verse or passage to rise up from the inside and counsel you.

For example, as I was preparing to minister one weekend during our three Sunday morning services, I was confident that I had God's specific word and direction for our congregants. Nevertheless, the night before I was to minister, I began struggling with an unsettling feeling of being disconnected from the Holy Spirit. My first thought was, *This must be spiritual warfare.* So I went into commando-style spiritual warfare prayer by speaking fiercely in tongues, binding Satan and his demons, then breaking word curses and witchcraft—all with no breakthrough.

The next morning, I was still frustrated and struggling to feel connected with the Holy Spirit. I told myself with exasperation, *I guess I'll just have to "faith-it" then!* With that, I carried on and did what most preacher women do on Sunday mornings: I prayed in tongues even more, blasted some worship music loudly, and prepared my family and myself to go to church. As I stood in front of the mirror, putting on my lashes and brows, there was a sudden clarity from the written Word already planted within my own heart. This verse rose up on the inside of me and seemingly turned the lights on: "Looking carefully lest anyone fall short of the grace of God; lest any root of bitterness springing up cause trouble, and by this many become defiled" (Hebrews 12:15).

Right there, I lifted my hands up high and spoke out loud to God and to myself in the mirror. I said to Him quite directly, "Do you want to know what my problem is?" As if He did not know. I said it one more time, but with force. "Do you want to know what my problem is?" And then I answered my own question. "My problem is that I'm bitter!" An undercurrent of bitterness had crept into my heart, and I was not aware of it until that exact moment. I repented immediately and felt a glorious reconnection with the Spirit once again. This all took place because I had the written Word planted in my heart, and it spoke up and shed light on my own heart at just the right time.

A prophetic person cannot be bitter. Bitterness distorts the sweet voice of the Lord and then misrepresents it. For instance, God will speak His endorsement to you about someone, but bitterness will do a voice-over and condemn them instead. If you prophesy out of a place bitterness, you will defile the person whom God intends to edify. Jesus described, "Blessed are the pure in heart, for they shall see God" (Matthew 5:8). Those who build themselves in the written Word continuously will discern His voice much more accurately because they have prepared their hearts for it.

Begin to Prophesy Using Scriptures

Some of the most powerful prophecies I have ever received, heard and given have been prophetic words that incorporated Bible verses and passages as the Holy Spirit gave guidance. This book that you hold in your hands came about because prophet and author James Goll prophesied to me on December 5, 2017. He began this unforgettable prophetic word by first disclosing the exact Scriptures that I pray almost daily over myself, specifically, "Create in me a clean heart, O God" (Psalm 51:10) and "Who may ascend into the hill of the LORD? Or who may stand in His holy place? He who has clean hands and a pure heart" (Psalm 24:3–4). Then he revealed God's intended future for my life, specifically that I would be a leading trainer in "prophetic wisdom." My editor at Chosen Books just happened to catch the replay of this prophetic word online and acted on it, which has developed into the book you are reading now.

With that said, are you ready to begin prophesying? I believe now is the perfect time to pause and receive this supernatural ability from the Holy Spirit if you do not already have it.

We already know from the Bible that all true prophecy comes from the Holy Spirit and that He has come to the entire Church, meaning those who believe in Jesus, to give you power from on high,[4] along with the special ability to prophesy. As I mentioned in chapter 1, to receive the gift of prophecy you can either ask for it from the Holy Spirit directly or you can have someone who has this ability to lay his or her hands on you and impart it to you through prayer. Derek Prince wrote that the laying on of hands is both a doctrine of the Church and "an act in which one person lays his hands upon the body of another person, with some definite spiritual purpose. Normally this act is accompanied either by prayer, a prophetic utterance, or both."[5]

Remember Paul's strong exhortation to us to "desire spiritual gifts, but especially that you may prophesy" (1 Corinthians

14:1). I have personally witnessed that this gift has the most permission on it out of any other supernatural gifts. In other words, if you truly desire to prophesy, without reserve the Holy Spirit will anoint you to do so.

Now pray this prayer with me (and I am praying this prayer for you):

Holy Spirit, I desire to prophesy! I ask You to give me Your supernatural ability to not only perceive Your voice, but to speak and prophesy as You lead me to do so. Help me to prophesy accurately. Help me to prophesy with impact! Thank You for hearing me. I receive Your gift by faith, now. In Jesus' name, Amen.

Just wait a few moments and breathe Him in. Allow the breath of the Holy Spirit to fill your lungs and to fill you from head to toe. Now it is time to prophesy, and I am going to lead you in a prophetic activation to help you get started.

Prophetic Activation Exercise

Look at your favorite passage of Scripture such as Psalm 23 or Psalm 91. As you look at the verses one by one, ask the Holy Spirit to highlight one or more of the verses to you. You will know His voice because it will stand out more than the others or seem as if it has His breath or His power on it.

Next, ask Him who needs this verse or these verses today. You will either hear a name, see a face in your imagination or have a strong leaning on the inside of you toward someone.

Go ahead and test this out. Call, text or message the person to say you were thinking and praying about him or her, then share the verse you believe He showed you. You could even follow it up with "Does that mean anything to you?" Or "Is there anything specific you need prayer for today?" And see how he or she responds.

This is how we begin. By taking a small step and taking a risk. As you keep doing that, before you know it, you will be taking bigger and bigger leaps of faith as you learn through experience how to distinguish His voice and prophetic word with more and more clarity.

Kingdom Principles

1. Perceiving the Holy Spirit's prophetic word begins with first perceiving His voice.
2. He does not always speak with enunciated sentence clarity. His voice can come as a feeling, an internal sound, an identifiable thought and a whole lot more.
3. A lifestyle in the written Word sifts and washes our inner thoughts and intentions, the very stuff that colors over His pure voice or blocks it out altogether.
4. When God trusts you with people, He entrusts you with more information about people. Maturing prophetic voices have learned to not say everything that is revealed.
5. To receive the gift of prophecy you can either ask for it from the Holy Spirit directly or you can have someone who has this ability to lay his or her hands on you and impart it to you through prayer.

Thoughts for Reflection

1. Can you remember the first time you perceived God's voice? How did His voice come to you?
2. Have you ever considered the relationship between your heart attitudes and your ability to identify His voice

accurately? What heart attitudes is He healing within you in this season?

3. How would you describe your activity and study of the written Word? How has this "washed" your attitudes and helped you to distinguish His voice more precisely?

4. When someone gives you a responsibility or directive through a prophetic word, how would you know if it is God or not? How should you respond when it is not God and the person giving the word insists that it is?

5. Have you ever sought the Holy Spirit for a prophetic word just using the Scriptures as your tool? If so, what were the results?

The Spirit of Wisdom

D r. Dave Williams, founder and retired senior pastor of Mount Hope Church in Lansing, Michigan, had an astonishing, trancelike vision in his early days of pastoring. He wrote:

I was laying on the bed. It was 10:30 p.m. Suddenly, I was caught into another world it seemed. Though I heard nothing verbally, I understood everything clearly through some form of nonverbal communication. I knew everything that was taking place. I could identify things even though nothing was being said to me in my ear.

In a flash, I was caught up off of the bed, and I realized I was in Lansing, Michigan. I saw an evil, hideous, horrible-looking creature hovering over Lansing. It frightened me for a moment. I was startled. It was breathtaking to see this ghastly creature hovering over my city. I noticed that this evil personality, which I somehow recognized as a principality (Ephesians 6:12) holding an enormous fine mesh net, guarding it jealously. It was a bulging, monstrous net that he was holding over Lansing.

I gazed into that net and saw thousands of people squirming around.[1]

Then he had a second vision, just as astonishing as the first:

I was in a room with a woman trying to give birth. She was laboring, and I was there helping. I would say, "*Push, push.*" And she would labor and travail and sweat, but the baby didn't want to come. I continued encouraging her, "*Push, push, push.*" The baby didn't want to come out, but finally, the head popped out, and I thought, "*Oh, that's wonderful! Now let's get the rest of the baby out. Push!*" And the woman would groan and struggle and push and labor and travail. I was worn out myself from helping this woman.

Finally, the baby came out, and I breathed a sigh of relief. Now the baby was out, and I noticed this woman looked like she hadn't labored at all. She just sat there when unexpectedly another baby came out! Then another and another. Soon they began coming out so fast that it almost looked like they were coming out two and three at a time.

There were babies all over the place. Babies, babies, everywhere babies![2]

The Holy Spirit often speaks to us from the written Word, with a personal word or through various impressions and thoughts. He also uses an extensive picture vocabulary to communicate His heart and plans to us, namely through visions and dreams. Visions come in several forms, from still pictures and short, quick movies that He will fix upon your imagination to powerful trances such as what you read here. Dr. Williams had been given powerful prophetic insight about the future through two highly symbolic visions. These visions came in a stronger dimension, something that a Christian might experience only a few times over the course of his or her life, if at all, which is a biblical pattern.

Realize that trances alter your reality as they are happening and bring a significant change to your life because they are so powerful. That is why I suspect spiritual error in most, but not all, who claim to have these kinds of trances all the time, because they are almost too strong for the mind and body to process. They also need to be worked out in prayer, interpreted back to you by the Holy Spirit and then submitted to the course of wise counsel.

Here is where we need to revisit the concept of prophetic wisdom and will do so throughout this chapter. Again, prophetic wisdom is not human wisdom, but supernatural wisdom that comes from the Holy Spirit. Many consider it unwise to take action on a vision, especially those of this magnitude, without proper interpretation and prophetic wisdom. If Dr. Williams did not engage those steps, he would not have been able to respond effectively to God's plans for the future.

Dr. Williams was keenly aware that those powerful visions contained strategic keys for God's intended ministry in Lansing, Michigan. Right after the first two visions, he received a third one. Here he felt as if he had been transported through the air from his hotel room in Chicago to their recently purchased forty acres of land in Lansing, Michigan. They had purchased the land to build a soul-winning center and planned to name it Mount Hope Church. What he saw in the vision was the actual facility being built on the property, and he heard the voice of the Lord with such an "intensity of love" that it melted him on the spot.

The Holy Spirit said with clarity, *Dave, look at what I am doing!* As he meditated on this one statement, the whole vision came together. "God was telling me as the pastor what we had to do if He was going to build the church," he said. Dave further explained how their first mandate was to do warfare in prayer with the principalities and powers and rulers of darkness that were keeping people in bondage. Their second mandate was to labor together by sharing the pastor's ministry to the lost and by helping out in the church.

Dave Williams's visions were deeply spiritual, yet the prophetic wisdom revealed to him was a mix of both the spiritual and pragmatic. The spiritual application involved prayer and engaging in spiritual warfare, of course. The pragmatic application was reaching out to those who do not believe in Christ, sharing the Gospel with them, discipling them and then encouraging them to serve faithfully in the church. These were his next steps, and something he communicated with regularity to all of his congregants. Together they carried out his visions, and a vibrant Mount Hope Church emerged that has impacted the city and the globe ever since.

How Trances Bring Significant Change

In Acts 10, both Cornelius and Peter experienced trancelike visions that brought distinct change to the relationship between Christian Jews and Gentiles, finally uniting them both in Christ. Cornelius, a Roman centurion, was God-fearing and devout. Being a Gentile meant he was not Jewish and was categorized as unclean and mostly unapproachable by the Jews, even Christian Jews. Regardless, Cornelius was visited by one of God's holy angels in a vision, and the angel gave him specific instructions. "Now send men to Joppa, and send for Simon whose surname is Peter. He is lodging with Simon, a tanner, whose house is by the sea. He will tell you what you must do" (verses 5–6).

Soon after, Peter also experienced a trance and saw all sorts of animals before him considered unclean to eat by him and his fellow Jews. He heard God's firm instruction: "Rise Peter, kill and eat!" As he questioned these new instructions, God spoke back to him, saying, "What God has cleansed you must not call common" (verse 15), and the vision ended. As Peter pondered the meaning of this vision, Cornelius's servants appeared to Peter in Joppa and told him about their angelic visitation, then invited him to speak to Cornelius. Peter went with them, and upon finding Cornelius he shared the Gospel with him, which resulted in Cornelius and his household becoming the first Gentile converts to Christianity.

The inclusion of Gentiles into the plan of salvation was prophesied centuries beforehand by the prophet Isaiah, only it was not communicated how that would happen until it came to pass.[3] In just the right time, the Holy Spirit released powerful visions coupled with prophetic wisdom—specific instructions through the angel that ultimately shifted the boundary lines of salvation in Christ to include every tribe, tongue and nation.

As powerful as these trances were to both Cornelius and Peter, they could have been rendered useless unless joined with prophetic wisdom. Cornelius was given that wisdom, meaning the specific steps to follow, but Peter did not receive any of the steps. Peter, then, was left to ponder the meaning of the trance until prophetic wisdom presented itself through Cornelius's servants as they relayed the angel's instructions. If Peter was too closed minded, however, he still might have rejected their initial instructions.

I believe it was the anointing released upon him through this powerful trance that gave him the ability to receive and act on their words in that season. We see later, however, how Peter digressed from the Lord's instructions by not associating with Gentiles while with certain Jews, an error addressed publicly and to his face by the apostle Paul.[4]

It is one thing to receive such a powerful vision of the future, but a whole different thing to walk out a supernatural vision successfully. With that said, let's discover more about the Spirit of wisdom and how to join His wisdom with the prophetic.

Defining the Spirit of Wisdom

The Bible reveals seven unique manifestations of the Holy Spirit. We see this in Isaiah 11:1–2:

> There shall come forth a Rod from the stem of Jesse, and a Branch shall grow out of his roots. The Spirit of the LORD shall rest upon Him, the Spirit of wisdom and understanding, the Spirit of counsel and might, the Spirit of knowledge and of the fear of the LORD.

These are not seven different spirits, but one Holy Spirit manifested in seven different dimensions—the Spirit of the Lord, wisdom, understanding, counsel, might, knowledge and the fear of the Lord. You can cross-reference this passage with other Bible passages to understand this more fully. For example, John wrote:

> To the seven assemblies (churches) that are in Asia: May grace (God's unmerited favor) be granted to you and spiritual peace (the peace of Christ's kingdom) from Him Who is and Who was and Who is to come, and from the seven Spirits [the sevenfold Holy Spirit] before His throne. . . . And from the throne preceded lightnings and thunderings, and voices. Seven lamps of fire were burning before the throne, which are the seven Spirits of God.
>
> Revelation 1:4 AMPC; 4:5 AMP

Pastor Chris Oyakhilome, in his book *The Seven Spirits of God*, mentioned this in reference to Revelation 1:4. He wrote, "This verse is quite striking. It's not talking about seven separate personalities, but seven separate and independent manifestations of the Holy Spirit in the life of the believer, which is indicative of the fullness of the Spirit."[5]

Have you ever considered what it really means to live in the fullness of the Spirit? For example, we are charged by the apostle Paul in Ephesians 5:18 to not be "drunk with wine," but to be "filled with the Spirit."

I have heard this passage preached many times, but all pointed toward one particular manifestation of the Spirit that looks like actual drunkenness, often combined with uncontrollable laughter. This is a biblical experience and something first observed with the 120 believers in the book of Acts just after the Holy Spirit fell upon them with astounding power.[6] If, then, Paul has charged us to be filled with the Spirit, we can conclude that we are not always filled with the Spirit.

If you are a believer in Jesus, the Holy Spirit does abide in you continuously, but that is not the same as walking in the fullness of the Spirit. I believe that experiencing the fullness of the Spirit involves the Spirit of the Lord coming and resting upon you, but then also embraces these six other powerful dimensions of the Spirit, including the Spirit of wisdom. Other ministers and authors have described the seven Spirits of God as being angelic beings, citing personal encounters and visions as the source of their revelation.

Fiorella Giordano, a prophet from Dallas, Texas, shared with me her personal encounter with a spirit of wisdom, actually an angel, who described himself as having charge over creativity, innovation, wealth and the paths of justice. The Bible does reveal the activity of angels as being of a wide variety and that they are sent to help those who are heirs to salvation, which is you and I who believe in Jesus Christ. We also read throughout the Bible how angels were sent to protect, guide, strengthen, reveal the future, provide and on and on.

Still, I would argue that the passages in Isaiah and the book of Revelation are in reference to seven personalities of the Holy Spirit, but that is not to say that angels would never be commissioned to co-labor on behalf of the Holy Spirit for such purposes. Either way, I am not looking to the angels for wisdom or any of the other dimensions listed, but to the Holy Spirit.

Nevertheless, should an angel appear, I receive from God's ministering spirits wholeheartedly, knowing that I am responsible to test the angelic message for congruency with written Scriptures.

The passages we read in Revelation that corresponded with Isaiah 11:1–2 described the seven Spirits of God as being before His throne in heaven. These seven Spirits do not remain in heaven, however, but go out into our physical world. We read in Revelation 5:6: "And I looked, and behold, in the midst of the throne and of the four living creatures, and in the midst of the elders, stood a Lamb as though it had been slain, having seven horns and seven eyes, which are the seven Spirits of God sent out into all the earth."

James Goll asked this probing question in one of his teaching videos: "How are the seven Spirits carried into the entire world?" He answered, saying, "This occurs as Spirit-filled believers in Christ Jesus carry the fullness of His radiating presence everywhere they go."[7] You and I can carry the fullness of His Spirit, but it helps to understand what that can look like, although the possibilities can be as endless as God Himself.

For the purposes of this chapter, I want to bring an emphasis to the Spirit of wisdom. The fullness of the Spirit of wisdom is accessible to the believer whenever needed, if not continuously. James wrote this bold statement: "If any of you lacks wisdom, let him ask of God, who gives to all liberally and without reproach, and it will be given to him" (James 1:5). And Proverbs 1:20 asserts, "Wisdom shouts in the streets. She cries out in the public square" (NLT). Still, we can all point to situations and seasons in our lives that were not marked with wisdom. Wisdom was available to us, only we did not tap in to it, or we rejected it for a variety of reasons. The truth is, we have the capacity to always respond well to life and to our prophetic words, because wisdom has been made obtainable. We can all walk in the fullness of wisdom by the Spirit of the Lord.

Carrying the Fullness of the Spirit

Pastor Tony Kim and his wife, Jessica, are the senior leaders of Renaissance Church in Bakersfield, California. Tony is the founder and leader of Roar Collective, an international network of transformational leaders, and the director for Harvest International Ministry in the United States, which is an apostolic network for revival, reformation and the transformation of nations. He also is a sought-out consultant for political leaders who want his reformational principles that transform communities as well as business leaders seeking to increase profitability.

Tony's powerful testimony includes how he was a miserably poor student and became involved in drugs and Asian gangs by age ten. Tony almost dropped out of school in junior high because "I had no purpose. I wasn't book smart at all." Tony's extended relatives were all very intelligent and highly educated, while Tony was advised to consider community college, if anything at all.

But things began to change after Tony became a true believer in Jesus Christ at a youth camp the summer after his eighth-grade year. "It started with a dream and in that dream, Jesus appeared to me and showed me I would preach the Gospel with power." Tony did not want to preach the Gospel at all and sought the Lord to prove Himself with another dream. He dreamt again that night, only more specifically. In the second dream, he was preaching in stadiums with salvations, deliverances and healings taking place. As a result of these two dreams and then a powerful vision of Jesus the very next day, Tony gave his life to Christ wholeheartedly, and he eventually found his way into full-time ministry.

Almost seventeen years later, Tony had another dream that joined his life in an unusual way to the Spirit of wisdom. He explained, "I dreamt about a young, golden-haired girl who

pleaded with me to not reject her because she had been 'rejected by all the others.'" In the dream, Tony gave the little
girl a hug and found out her name was Sophia. As I had mentioned in the first chapter, *sophia* is a Greek word that means
"wisdom," [8] more specifically, supernatural wisdom. Judging
by her name, Tony knew he had been given a supernatural invitation to receive the Spirit of wisdom. As he sought the Lord
in prayer, he had a second dream again with the young girl Sophia who gave him the charge to "cross over" into the tangible
activity of supernatural wisdom. Within a month, he found
himself being invited into conversations by local government
leaders on how to transform communities, and it took off from
there.

"I don't feel any different," Tony said. "It's like I just know
the right thing to say in these conversations, and leaders recognize that what I'm saying is coming from somewhere. It's
just not natural wisdom." Tony continues to be sought out
by government and business leaders in the United States and
abroad for strategic counsel about social and economic matters.

Wisdom Is Not Passive

The biggest mistake I see people make when they receive a genuine prophetic word, either directly from the Lord or through
another person, is failing to steward that word into fullness.
Naturally speaking, if you know you need to do something
and you neglect it, that is not wisdom. If you know you need
to study for an exam and you do not set aside time to study,
that is not wisdom. If you know you need to pay attention to
a family matter and you ignore it, that is not wisdom. Wisdom
is not passive, but active.

Jesus went to teach the Word of God by Lake Gennesaret but
was hindered by the great throng of people who were pressing

in to hear Him. He noticed a few empty fishing boats on the shoreline and stepped into one, asking the owner to push it out from the shoreline. The boat owner's name was Simon Peter, and once in the boat and away from shore, Jesus could communicate more effectively to the large crowd. When He had finished speaking, Jesus turned to Peter and prophesied. He said, "Launch out into the deep and let down your nets for a catch" (Luke 5:4). Here Jesus revealed the future. There was going to be a "catch" of fish, as long as Peter let down his nets. Peter "answered and said to Him, 'Master, we have toiled all night and caught nothing; nevertheless at Your word I will let down the net.' And when they had done this, they caught a great number of fish, and their net was breaking" (verses 5–6).

Did you notice here that Jesus told Peter to let down his nets (plural), but Peter responded by letting down only a single net?

Here is a lesson in prophetic wisdom. How we listen and how we respond to a prophetic word determines how we will receive. Peter was given a clear prophetic word and instructions on how to proceed. After a disappointing night, he heard the prophetic word and instructions of Jesus and acted on it, only he acted on it passively and reduced the outcome. We can all learn from this. Either way, the miracle catch of fish and the breaking "net" still impacted Peter so greatly that he left everything behind to follow Jesus.

In contrast with Peter's passivity, pastor and songwriter Simone Benoit Bracken took action when I prophesied to her at one of my conferences. Simone has a unique sound and has led worship for several years at her church and at various events and conferences. During the evening session, you could feel the atmosphere of heaven permeate the room as she led in worship. I noticed that all of my senses were heightened under the heavy presence of the Lord. We were both standing on my church platform, her leading in worship and me just waiting on the Spirit, when I turned toward her, and words began tumbling out of my mouth. I said something like, "There you go! You are elevating and stepping onto big platforms."

Six months later, Simone was recording her first album, *Journey of Pursuit*, in Redding, California. While recording, she received a phone call from one of the biggest stars in the history of the MMA. They knew each through a mutual friendship, and he called asking her for suggestions for a walk-out song at his next UFC fight. Simone shared, "I told him about my song 'Risk,' and to my shock he wanted me to come the next month to the Kansas City basketball arena and perform it live."

Here is where Simone needed prophetic wisdom, not human wisdom, and then not to be passive with whatever the Holy Spirit said to do. "I'm a pastor," she said. "And these kinds of fights are totally secular and host an insanely demonic atmosphere." It was definitely a gray area. If Simone agreed, she would be the first live performance during a walk-out and doing so in front of thirty thousand attendees and a million-plus television viewers. She felt that loving push from the Holy Spirit to proceed and knew she needed to be ready in prayer more than anything else.

"These two fighters, including the audience, were channeling a sick rage and anger into the atmosphere," Simone explained. "I felt God's secure protection in that environment, only the clash of kingdoms was beyond anything I have experienced before." In the end, Simone did the live performance and received a global spread of emails and messages from people who were in tears from the song she sang, including people from that night's arena. "They didn't have language to describe the transforming touch of the Holy Spirit because they were unchurched, but I could reach them for Jesus in that moment."

Her performance went so well that she was invited to perform again, only in a much bigger arena in Houston, Texas.

Once again, her live performance brought her global attention and much opportunity to share the Gospel.

How to Access the Spirit of Wisdom

In the beginning of Solomon's reign, God appeared in the night and commanded Solomon, "Ask! What shall I give you?" (2 Chronicles 1:7). Solomon replied by asking God for wisdom so he could lead and judge well. The Lord, well pleased with his request, said in verses 11–12:

> "Because this was in your heart, and you have not asked riches or wealth or honor or the life of your enemies, nor have you asked long life—but have asked wisdom and knowledge for yourself, that you may judge My people over whom I have made you king—wisdom and knowledge are granted to you; and I will give you riches and wealth and honor, such as none of the kings have had who were before you, nor shall any after you have the like."

Solomon became the wisest man on earth through super-natural means, as visibly demonstrated in his decisions, organization, architecture, wealth and much more. How did Solomon attain this level of wisdom? He simply asked for it.

Much like the gift of prophecy, there is ample access and grace to receive prophetic wisdom. Here it is again: "If any of you lacks wisdom, let him ask of God, who gives to all liberally and without reproach, and it will be given to him" (James 1:5). This kind of wisdom was so critical to the success of the early Church that the apostle Paul prayed specifically for the believers in Ephesus to receive "the spirit of wisdom and revelation" (Ephesians 1:17).

Do you want to walk in this kind of wisdom? Are you in need of prophetic wisdom? The key to receive is to ask for it. And God will give you a full supply, because His prophetic wisdom is always accessible and never stops speaking to us (see Proverbs 8).

You have now been equipped with the fundamentals of the gift of prophecy and prophetic wisdom. In this next chapter, you will be stretched to know that you have been given a set of spiritual eyes to see in the spiritual realm, something most people do not believe they have or do not know how to step into.

Kingdom Principles

1. The Holy Spirit often speaks to us from the written Word, with a personal word, or through various impressions and thoughts. He also uses an extensive picture vocabulary to communicate His heart and plans to us, namely through visions and dreams.

2. Trances are a more powerful kind of vision and only come sometimes. Trances will bring significant change to your life and require prayer, proper interpretation and prophetic wisdom to be carried out successfully.

3. Much like the gift of prophecy, there is ample access and grace to receive prophetic wisdom. When we walk in the fullness of the Spirit, we will walk in the Spirit of wisdom (see Ephesians 5:8; Isaiah 11:1–2).

4. The biblical key to accessing the Spirit of wisdom is to ask for it. When you ask God for wisdom, He will give you a full supply (see James 1:5).

5. The biggest mistake people make when they receive a genuine prophetic word is passivity. Wisdom is not passive; it is active. Prophetic wisdom takes action steps once those steps are revealed.

Thoughts for Reflection

1. Have you ever experienced the voice of God through a dream or vision, or even a trance? What happened as a result?

2. Have you ever considered that being filled with the fullness of the Spirit would also include being filled with the Spirit of wisdom? What does that look like in your life?

3. We have all had situations and seasons in our lives that were not marked with wisdom. If supernatural wisdom is always available, how did you miss accessing wisdom during that season?

4. Prophetic words require our stewardship. Do you have any prophetic words over your life that have gone neglected?

5. Do you need prophetic wisdom? Do you want to walk in this kind of wisdom? Take some time to ask the Holy Spirit to come upon you in the fullness of His wisdom.

Five

Anointed to See

*H*ave you ever heard someone say, "I can see into the spiritual realm," or, "I can see things"? I have had this ability for as long as I can remember, even years before I ever became a Christian. Perhaps you have experienced something similar. When I say that I could see into the spiritual realm, I am referring to a supernatural ability to see past your natural sight and to see and encounter spiritual realities that exist within the invisible realm that is all around us. Now that I look back and have more understanding, I realize that my initial ability as a child to see into the spiritual realm might not have come from the Holy Spirit, although certainly He can grace children this way if He so chooses.

Families steeped in Freemasonry or other occult practices, and mine was, often gain access intentionally or unintentionally to what is known as the "third eye." This is a supernatural ability to see into the spiritual realm, but not in partnership with the Holy Spirit. Sadly, this led to many demonic experiences, and such experiences did not balance out until after I gave my life to Christ as a freshman in college. After my salvation and once I became aware of this possibility, I repented of it and gave my spiritual eyes over to the Holy Spirit for His sanctified use. I continued to see a healthy amount of the demonic, but progressively I began to see angels, visions of heaven and Jesus, and more.

What Do You See?

When I was newly married and serving in ministry alongside my husband, the Holy Spirit began to teach me Himself how to see into the spiritual realm, mostly for the purposes of prophetic ministry and intercession. (Keep in mind, this was well before any credible teaching and discussion had been created for this kind of topic.) In my day-to-day routine, I found myself fixing my eyes on people I encountered, or the image of a person's face or a certain situation would fix strongly into my imagination, followed by the voice of the Holy Spirit asking me, *What do you see?* He was not referring to what I saw with my natural eyes. He was referring to my spiritual eyes. He was asking me to tell Him what could only be identified spiritually.

For example, let's say I ran into "Bob" at the grocery store. If Bob was someone I knew, typically I would have engaged in some light conversation before breaking off to finish my shopping. At this point I might have heard the voice of the Spirit ask me, *What do you see?* My response may have been *I see a dark cloud of depression over his head.* And then I would catch myself thinking through as to how I saw that, because I could not always describe how. I could see invisible information that was there, only it was not visible in the natural sense at all. Still, I saw it in my own mind or spirit, or I would feel it.

After a season of this kind of exchange, again and again, with the Holy Spirit, He added one more question. After He asked me, *What do you see?* and I responded, He asked me,

What do you know? Here again He was not referring to natural information, but spiritual information in connection with what I just saw. Going back to the example of Bob and then adding the follow-up question, I might have responded, *He's depressed because he lost his job.* Again and again, I found myself praying deeply into such outcomes. Compassion would rise up within me, and I would pray what I saw and knew, but keeping everything in private. To be honest, I kept wondering whether or not this was even real.

The Holy Spirit continued to lead me in this spiritual exercise for a few years before I realized that what I was seeing and knowing was far more accurate than I ever considered. For example, I kept starting conversations with people thinking they had told me specific and personal information, only to find out they never had told me anything. Somehow I had seen the information by the Holy Spirit, only I had not distinguished it as prophetic revelation. This got me into some trouble at first until people caught on that I had a prophetic gift and they had not been gossiped about.

Eventually I found the exchanges in the Bible between God and Jeremiah and then God and Amos. With both men, God asked them the same question He had been asking me: *What do you see?* These prophets saw specific pictures in the spiritual realm and described them back to God. Jeremiah said, "I see the branch of an almond tree," and then, "I see a boiling pot, and it is facing away from the North" (Jeremiah 1:11, 13). God responded, "You have seen well, for I am ready to perform My word," and then, "Out of the North calamity shall break forth" (verses 12–13). And when Amos said to the Lord that he saw a plumb line, the Lord responded, "Behold, I am setting a plumb line in the midst of My people Israel; I will not pass by them anymore" (Amos 7:8).

After reading these passages, which bolstered my confidence, I knew the Holy Spirit has been training people to see into the spiritual realm the exact same way for thousands of years. This ability comes from the Holy Spirit, and it comes with a clear biblical pathway.

Dreams and Visions—God's Picture Vocabulary

Most likely you have heard the saying, "A picture is worth a thousand words." Yet when God speaks to you using His picture vocabulary, referring to visions and dreams, these pictures carry dimensions of wonder and eternity that seem to go way beyond our finite language. Still, the Holy Spirit's imagery, once unpacked and articulated with prophetic wisdom, will superimpose an astonishing force of change over people and circumstances. These images do not form from our own imagination; they are visions sourced to the very imagination of God and encapsulated with power just waiting to be released. Visions vary in intensity and have a broad expression, including the ability to see in the spiritual realm.

Although there is controversy over the exact meaning and application of the term, some refer to the invisible realm as the "second heaven." The Bible does not use the exact phrase *second heaven*, but it is inferred nonetheless. In 2 Corinthians 12:1–2, we read Paul's description of being caught up to the third heaven, the place where God sits on His throne and where we will dwell permanently once we have ceased living on earth:

> It is doubtless not profitable for me to boast. I will come to visions and revelations of the Lord: I know a man in Christ who fourteen years ago—whether in the body I do not know, or whether out of the body I do not know, God knows—such a one was caught up to the third heaven.

Based on his reference, we can assume there must be a first and second heaven, and perhaps even more.

Most theologians believe that the first heaven is our natural world. There is more debate, however, about the location and contents of the second heaven. I believe the second heaven encompasses the space that exists between heaven and earth and is capable of hosting God's holy angels, but also some very real demons.[1] I base that on personal experience as well as what is written in the book of Daniel, namely that the demonic prince of Persia created some very real resistance to Daniel's angel that had been sent to him from God in response to his prayers (see Daniel 10). Again, visions come in many various forms of pictures, either still or moving. For example, the prophet Daniel saw powerful moving pictures about the future in both dreams and in real time, but then he also saw powerful visions within the confines of his own mind (see 7:1–2).

Seeing in the spiritual realm is another form of having visions. You will see angels, demons, the future, the present, the past and a whole lot more. At times I see both the natural and spiritual realm simultaneously, with the spiritual realm being superimposed over the natural.

Minister and prophet Jamie Galloway shared in an interview with Patricia King how he, too, began to see into the spiritual realm as a little kid, only it was overwhelming. "I had no one to talk to about this," he explained. Jamie grew up going to church, but his church did not believe or talk about the things he was experiencing. He went on to say, "I was seeing spiritual things, I didn't know what to do, and thought I was going absolutely crazy." According to Jamie, "This was the perfect setup for some very real sabotage from the enemy." At age seventeen, however, Jamie made a commitment to follow Christ and began to see into the spiritual realm on a much different level. He began hearing and seeing angels and having vivid and wild heavenly encounters, just to name a few. Since then, he has authored several books and ministered around the globe, all because he had been anointed by the Holy Spirit "to see."[2]

I have heard from many people who began to see the spiritual realm as young children, but many said it was a negative experience because they were not in Christian homes or did not have any support. Shanna Gil from Harvest Church in Turlock, California, said, "I only saw spirits and ghosts as a child, but now as an adult Christian I see more angels." To clarify, Shanna explained that she knows ghosts are actually demons, but that is the only word she had to describe them at that age. Similarly, Chantal Giannopoulos, from Adelaide, Australia, remarked that her ability to see spiritually as a child was "quite scary." She had her turnaround after becoming a Christian and renouncing her agreement with the occult "third eye" during a personal prayer session with a prayer counselor. Now she is in a supportive church environment and sees a lot more things pertaining to heaven and the angels, and not just the demonic. Finally, both Shanna and Chantal were able to resolve lingering issues and fears about seeing spiritually, and both are powerful intercessors and ministry leaders in their churches. This is not everyone's response, nonetheless.

Some have shut off their spiritual eyes in reaction to seeing demonic spirits, but the Holy Spirit wants you to know that "blessed are your eyes for they see" (Matthew 13:16). He wants to partner with you and train your spiritual eyes to see, but in a more balanced way. To that end, here are the biblical fundamentals to activate your spiritual eyes to see.

How to See in the Spiritual Realm

Whether you have always seen in the spiritual realm, you never have or you used to but no longer do, you can have your spiritual eyes activated to see more than you have before. What I am saying to you is not presumption or wishful thinking, but one of the promises and benefits of partnership with the Holy Spirit.

Here are three main keys to help you to see spiritually:

1. *Through the outpouring of the Holy Spirit*

We read in Acts 2:17 that prophecy, visions and dreams are preceded by the pouring out of the Holy Spirit upon your person: "And it shall come to pass in the last days, says God, that I will pour out of My Spirit on all flesh; your sons and your daughters shall prophesy, your young men shall see visions, your old men shall dream dreams." He already came to the believers in the Upper Room, first in the form of a mighty wind, and then He fell upon them as individual tongues of fire. He was then described as water poured out upon human flesh, and when He pours Himself on you, not only will you prophesy, but you will also see visions and dreams.

Coming under the outpouring of the Spirit is something you can seek Him for personally, or you can attend an anointed church or conference and experience an outpouring of the Spirit that way. When He pours out on you, you will feel His presence and most likely exhibit some kind of manifestation that you did. Either way, know that your eyes will be opened to the spiritual realm and you will see with the eyes of the Spirit of God.

And then there was Stephen, a deacon in the first church of Jerusalem who served as part of a team of seven men to oversee a benevolence ministry. Stephen, a notable evangelist "full of faith and power, did great wonders and signs among the people" (Acts 6:8). He also made history as the first martyr of the Christian Church. On his last and most eventful day on earth, Stephen, "being full of the Holy Spirit, gazed into heaven and saw the glory of God, and Jesus standing at the right hand of God, and said, 'Look! I see the heavens opened and the Son of Man standing at the right hand of God!'" (7:55–56). Again, there is a connection with the outpouring of the Spirit and seeing into the spiritual realm.

Later in the New Testament, the apostle John beheld and wrote out a powerful vision, which became the book of Revelation.

Notice how he was positioned when he saw all of these things. He was in the Spirit, meaning he was overshadowed by the presence of God, and here he saw many aspects of heaven and the future through the eyes of the Spirit. We read his description: "I was in the Spirit on the Lord's Day, and I heard behind me a loud voice, as of a trumpet, saying, 'I am the Alpha and the Omega, the First and the Last,' and, 'What you see, write in a book'" (Revelation 1:10–11). You will notice that nearly every chapter of Revelation contains the words *I saw*.

The late Ruth Ward Heflin, a powerful intercessor and minister who led scores of people into encounters with the Holy Spirit, often shared about her visions of heaven and would prophesy the things she saw. She described in her book *Glory— Experiencing the Atmosphere of Heaven* that originally she heard the voice of the Lord clearly but was not one to see visions. Still, she was thrilled to hear what others saw in the spiritual realm, yet believing this supernatural ability was a blessing relegated to the few. After "Susan," an Episcopalian, started having visions from the moment she was filled with the Spirit, Susan challenged Ruth on her belief that she did not see anything. She pointed out that when Ruth prophesied, she often said, "I see this" or "I see that" as she prophesied. Ruth then recognized it was true. She had been seeing into the spiritual realm all along. This flowed with so much ease within her that it did not register with her that she had supernatural endowment that had emerged in the midst of her many encounters with the Holy Spirt.[3]

Is this you? I have found many saints to be seeing in the spiritual realm, only they did not know it. For example, let's say you drove past a homeless person requesting assistance with a sign, but you passed them by for a lot of good reasons. In your mind's eye, however, you watched a quick movie of yourself driving to a nearby fast-food restaurant or something similar and then buying a meal for them. Let me point something out to you. Did you know you just had a vision? What you experienced was an actual directive from the Spirit, only you did not recognize it as such because it was so quick and without much emotion. Pay attention to the pictures in your head, especially when you feel His presence in a heightened way. He is speaking to you and has been all along.

2. Through prayer

How would I describe prayer? Prayer is like breathing and becomes oxygen to our spirit. Prayer is a two-way communication and always a supernatural exchange. In the place of prayer is where heaven and earth meet and we experience deep communion with the Holy Spirit. In prayer, we offer our sweet worship, petitions and a heart that leans in to His. In prayer, He offers His felt love, His perfect wisdom, and tells us the things to come. Prayer is daily and necessary, as God does nothing without our petition and partnership. When we pray, God will awaken our spiritual eyes to see what He sees so we can do what He is doing.

Cornelius, the notable Roman centurion in the Bible, was a generous man and known for continuous prayer (see Acts 10:2). As I had mentioned in the previous chapter, Cornelius encountered an angel in a vision who gave him a specific set of instructions that led him and his household to become the first Gentile converts to Christianity. Cornelius saw the angel with his own eyes. He dialogued with him, much like you would dialogue with a human being. Cornelius was a man of great prayer, and his eyes were opened to the spiritual realm. This not only changed his life and his family's, too, but it opened the door to salvation in Christ to every nationality, not just the Jews.

Jesus, too, engaged in significant amounts of prayer. He rose up early to pray while it was still dark and spent entire nights in prayer communing with our heavenly Father (see Mark 1:35;

Luke 6:12). He also reflected a passionate and vibrant dialogue with God, one that teaches us to have emotions and expression in prayer. We read, "During the days of Jesus' life on earth, he offered up prayers and petitions with loud cries and tears to the one who could save him from death, and he was heard because of his reverent submission" (Hebrews 5:7 NIV). We also see that He was fully obedient to the leading of His Father, but pay attention as to how He was led. He described it like this: "The Son can do nothing of Himself, but what He sees the Father do; for whatever He does, the Son also does in like manner" (John 5:19).

What does this mean? I believe Jesus was seeing in the spiritual realm as He prayed and received His strategic battle plans for each day through visions. Notice that Jesus never wasted a day, never got on the wrong boat and never made a mistake. He was always in perfect step with His Father because He saw and obeyed His instructions seen in the place of prayer.

My husband and I have two wonderful children, a boy and a girl. Perhaps you did not know that I am physically unable to have children. Regardless, the Holy Spirit saw fit to show me both of my children in two separate visions well ahead of time. I saw their gender and heard their names as He prepared our home for a miracle. He really does know us in His heart before we are born, and He knew my children before they ever came into being (see Jeremiah 1:5). Despite my physical limitations, eventually I became pregnant, and both children arrived just as He promised and were born five years apart. I also became pregnant a third time, but lost the pregnancy through miscarriage. I was devastated and experienced a deep grief that gnawed at me for years.

I prayed diligently through this problem and eventually was taken to heaven in a vision. While there, I saw a beautifully dressed young girl playing with a group of other beautifully attired children. I knew in my heart that she was my daughter whom I had miscarried on earth. She also knew who I was. Grabbing my hand excitedly, she said, "I can't wait to hear you tell me the stories about you, the ones I've already read about." I knew what she was referring to. I had read in Psalm 139:16 about the book God wrote about your life before you were ever born. Apparently, she had read my book, and at this point I sort of lost myself. I asked her, "Do you want me to just come over now?" She replied, "No. You're not finished yet." And then the vision ended.

I want to assure you that this was not some kind of necromancy. I did not conjure this up or even expect it. Clearly, I was in heaven and saw many children who had died on earth but were alive in Christ. That is important to clarify because in their grief some might try to contact the dead, and that is scripturally off-limits (see Leviticus 20:6; Isaiah 8:19). I believe Jesus allowed this heavenly encounter at a key time in my life so at last I could resolve the ongoing grief I felt and be encouraged to finish my race, because I am not finished yet. This vision took place in prayer, the place where He opens our spiritual eyes to see realities we could not see otherwise.

3. *Through the doorway of the Word*

I discovered this key to seeing in the spiritual realm by divine accident, or more accurately by divine setup. As I mentioned in chapter 3, I was deeply hungry to know and understand the written Word of God and spent much time studying it. I had also learned the distinct blessing that coincides with knowing and observing God's Word after reading His clear counsel to Joshua: "This Book of the Law shall not depart from your mouth, but you shall meditate in it day and night, that you may observe to do according to all that is written in it. For then you will make your way prosperous, and then you will have good success" (Joshua 1:8).

Joel Osteen, pastor of Lakewood Church in Houston, Texas, defined in his blog what it means to meditate on Scriptures. He wrote, "To meditate simply means to reflect on the same thing over and over again, visualize it and let the meaning of it sink deep down into your heart."[4] That is what I was doing. I was meditating on His Word and letting His Word sink deeply inside of me.

On one particular day, I was meditating on the fascinating truths in Psalm 8, and then something powerful happened. As I read over and over, "What is man that You are mindful of him, and the son of man that You visit him?" (verse 4), suddenly my spiritual eyes opened. I could see my natural surroundings, but I could see my spiritual surroundings at the same time. I saw Jesus standing right in front of me, and out of my mouth came this: "You've been there all along, haven't You!" He nodded in affirmation, and this verse flashed across my mind: "I will never leave you nor forsake you" (Hebrews 13:5). He is always with us, only we do not see Him unless our spiritual eyes are opened to it. At the same time, I was left in a place of wonder, having realized the written Scriptures in and of themselves are so powerful they can serve as a doorway into the realm of visions. His written Word is alive, not just dead words on the page.

Do you want to know how to utilize this key? You, too, can use the written Word to see into the spiritual realm. I like using the Scriptures to step into this because the Word keeps you anchored and sound, and it keeps your eyes directed toward Him. Here is an activation exercise to help you.

Seeing in the Spiritual Realm Activation Exercise

In the gospels Jesus spent time at specific locations. For example, He would walk by the Sea of Galilee, or He would go to the Mount of Olives to pray or teach His disciples (see Matthew 4:18; Luke 22:39). He also took a seat at Jacob's Well (see John 4:5–6). One website boasts that the Sea of Galilee has changed very little since Jesus called the four fisherman, and the Mount of Olives hosts many biblical scenes in the life of Jesus and history of the early Church. Begin to meditate on these scenes and imagine what it would be like to walk, sit and talk with Jesus. In your imagination, go to the Sea of Galilee, to the Mount of Olives or to Jacob's Well and put yourself next to Him. Ask the Holy Spirit to breathe on your imagination. At some point you will notice that your sanctified imagination begins to take on movement as you enter into the realm of visions. Here you can talk to Jesus and ask Him your specific questions. You will know if it is real or not by the way He answers you. He always answers in perfect harmony with His written Word. And He has a way of answering you with such uncanny wisdom that it could not be just your imagination.

There is actually one more key. When you align in heart and ministry with a seer prophet, more often than not you, too, will see into the spiritual realm. Seer prophets have a governing role in the Body of Christ and receive their prophetic instructions through visions, dreams and insight into the spiritual realm. They operate in heightened supernatural function, and when you come into proximity with prophets like this, you come under their covering, and their supernatural ability to see rubs off on you. I will explain more about prophets and different kinds of prophets in the next chapter.

As you venture deeper in this with the Holy Spirit, you will see many things in the spiritual realm, only you will not act on everything you see. That is the mistake some people make with this supernatural ability. Think about how this works in our natural world. When you enter a room, you see many things. You might see a table, some chairs, various décor items and some books perhaps. You do not do something with everything you see, but only focus on one or two tasks typically. It is the same with what you see in the spiritual realm. The Holy Spirit will point out to you what is important and what to ignore. He will take what you see and speak into its outcome, which is the prophetic word, and then give you prophetic wisdom to see it come to pass.

Kingdom Principles

1. Seeing in the spiritual realm is a supernatural ability to see past your natural sight and to see and encounter spiritual realities that exist within the invisible realm that is all around us.

2. Seeing the spiritual realm is another form of having visions. You will see angels, demons, the future, the present and past and a whole lot more.

3. People and families steeped in Freemasonry and other occult practices might have the supernatural ability to see spiritually, but it could be a demonic source. You can repent of this possibility and give your spiritual eyes over to the Holy Spirit for sanctified use.

4. The Holy Spirit might train you to see in the spiritual realm much like He did with prophets of old, asking you, *What do you see?* He is referring to what you see in the spiritual realm and not the natural.

5. You can see in the spiritual realm through the outpouring of the Holy Spirit, through prayer and through the doorway of the Word. You might also see spiritually by being aligned to a seer prophet.

Thoughts for Reflection

1. I believe the Holy Spirit is asking you and all of us, *What do you see?* If He were to ask you that right now, how would you respond?

2. Do you know how to come under the outpouring of the Holy Spirit personally, or do you have access to such in a corporate setting?

3. Have you ever seen still pictures, flowing pictures or different kinds of visions in your time of prayer or in connection to what you prayed about? Did you realize these were visions? Do you see these same kind of images when you are out and about in your day?

4. Have you ever had your spiritual eyes opened while meditating in the Word?

5. Have you ever prophesied out of the things you have seen in the spiritual realm. If not, what might that look like?

Six

Wisdom and Secrets
for Prophets

everal years ago, I had the most unusual vision during a conference at our downtown campus in Turlock, California. It was a trancelike vision, such as what I described earlier, the kind where your whole world disappears and you find yourself in another reality. Inside this vision, a human-sized pure-white angel with a man's face and form approached me from midair. He held in his hands a large scroll and a plume pen. The scroll appeared to be about four feet wide and ten feet long with writing on both the front and back sides.

I could not decipher the writing, but there was a space at the bottom of the scroll specially prepared to receive my signature. I am not sure how I knew this, but in the vision I understood within myself that I needed to sign the scroll. I also knew that my signature meant I had agreed to my call as a prophet to the nations. In the vision, the call as a prophet was crystal clear.

In real life, however, I had never considered this before or even aspired to it.

I told the angel, "I've signed your contract. Now what?"

"It's not a contract," he replied. "It's a covenant, and I'll be back."

As I came out of the vision, I realized I was lying flat on my back on the floor. I have no recollection as to how I ended up on the floor like that.

Above me, one of our conference speakers shouted enthusiastically in her French accent, "You are a prophet of God! You are called to the nations!"

Still, I did not know what to make of all this. *I'm a prophet now? What does that mean, and what do I do?* This vision yielded the beginnings of a new anointing and authority in my life, launching me into some mighty adventures in God as well as some shocking spiritual warfare. As I mentioned in chapter 4, these kinds of trances can shift the course of your life, as they did for me.

How Are Prophets Called?

I have revisited this vision in my heart many times since. On this side of things, I can see now that I had all the makings of a prophet—a divinely ordered wiring that lends itself toward the gift of prophecy, the discerning of spirits, deep intercession, a leadership gift and the propensity to train and equip others—only I did not know it. I say this humbly when I tell you the supernatural gifts and outworking of all this exhibited much stronger in my life than nearly everyone I knew. Maybe I would have deduced it at some point, but it still took a spiritual encounter to launch me into my calling as a prophet. Though every prophet's story is unique, in general here are some things to consider.

To clarify, the *gift of prophecy* is an anointing, meaning a supernatural ability, that comes from the Holy Spirit. We read in 1 Corinthians 12:7, "Now to each one the manifestation of the Spirit is given for the common good" (NIV). Then we see a listing of nine gifts of the Spirit in verses 8–10, which includes the gift of prophecy, before Paul's final point: "All these are the work of one and the same Spirit" (verse 11 NIV). Take note that Paul makes no connection here to indicate that those who prophesy by the Holy Spirit are automatically prophets, which is a common assumption that people make. If the ability to prophesy meant you were a prophet, then eventually we would become overpopulated with such persons in the Body of Christ, because this anointing is so accessible. Having the gift of prophecy, then, and being a prophet are simply not one and the same.

A prophet is called by Jesus Christ and not by the Holy Spirit. The office of the prophet is one of the five governing roles in the Body of Christ, and these roles are collectively referred to as the "fivefold ministry." According to Ephesians 4:11, Jesus Himself "gave some to be apostles, some prophets, some evangelists, and some pastors and teachers." According to Cindy Jacobs, prophet and founder of Generals International, "when Christ ascended, He took His whole ministry mantle, divided it, and gave it in five parts to men and women. All five are needed to perfect, mature and equip the saints."[1] The prophet, more specifically, does not just prophesy, but has a leadership role and much greater responsibility. Jacobs explained the differences like this: "The gift of prophecy is for edification, exhortation and comfort, whereas the prophet flows in areas of guidance, instruction, rebuke, judgment and revelation—whatever Christ chooses to speak for the purification and perfection of His church."[2]

Let me emphasize a key point from Ephesians 4:11: It is Jesus *Himself* who gives some people the gift of prophecy. Since the

Church is His Body, and He is the Head of the Church, then understandably He would be responsible to choose His governing team. There is a division of responsibilities between God the Father, God the Son and God the Holy Spirit, but still they flow as One and in perfect unity. With that said, if you are called as a prophet, then Jesus will make it abundantly clear that you are one. No human can call you into this office (although some might suspect it, and true prophets will often identify it by the Holy Spirit). You, yourself, cannot call yourself into this office, and I am certain you will not earn this role either. Only Jesus calls men and women as prophets, and all of them will say they were not qualified for it. He never calls the qualified, and every prophet will attest that He puts all those He has called through a rigorous training to prepare and equip them.

One such prophet is Michelle Passey from Washington State, who received her call as a prophet unexpectedly while serving as a cabin leader for a Christian high school camp in 2006. After a ministering guest challenged the students to seek the Lord and hear Him for their calling, she, too, heard clearly from Jesus that night. "I've called you as a prophet," He said.

"I was there to help the students, and wasn't there for myself," she said. "Obviously, God had a different plan for me." Her call as a prophet was unclear to her in its execution, but soon after, pastors and other leaders began to call her a prophet without any prompting. This was her supernatural confirmation.

As the years progressed, Michelle understood better what it means to be a prophet through reading books and listening to as much teaching as she could find from reputable prophets. She also traveled long distances and took the time to attend schools and conferences just to get a deeper understanding of the role of a prophet.

"The journey has been intensely hard at times and glorious at other times," she explained. "I was trained in the 'school' of the Holy Spirit as well as through other prophets." Years later, she is now a confirmed as a prophet by a wide variety of ministry leaders and recognized within the local church. Michelle spends most of her time training and equipping other prophets to hear the voice of God and to lead well.

The Processing of God's Prophets

Most of the prophets in the Bible seemed to emerge out of nowhere and from humble places. Moses, for example, left his lavish life in the Egyptian king's palace and lived humbly as a shepherd in the wilderness for forty years before emerging to deliver Israel. And then there was Amos, who was a lowly shepherd and farmer, and one not recognized by the more established prophets (see Amos 7:14–15). The unassuming Amos was sent by God to warn all of Israel and call them to repentance with just as much authority as the other prophets.

Elijah, in like manner, appeared from the backside of the desert to confront wicked King Ahab (see 1 Kings 17:1–7). "Elijah went through a season of testing and preparation, but that process is hidden from us," wrote J. Lee Grady, editor for *Charisma* magazine. He added, "True prophets will go through periods of hiddenness and intense brokenness. God must deal with pride, greed and self-centeredness. The prophet must also learn to live in a place of intimate fellowship with God where the praises of men don't affect him."[3]

Typically, prophets are held in obscurity until it is time for their public revealing. Living in the place of obscurity can feel as if you have been worked over in such a manner as to reveal every heart condition you can possibly have, both good and bad. This processing, which accumulates over a period of many years, is intended to reveal your true character and build integrity. If this is missed, ignored or bypassed, you might start out operating in the role of prophet but will not finish well.

Experience has shown me that God seems to care more about my heart than my platform and spectacular public ministry. In my own life, I remember a time of severe testing involving a group of prophets and pastors who were living impure lives during which I felt I was the only one with the guts to address the issue head-on. Feeling smugly self-righteous, I found myself in situations that seemed to surface my own impure heart motives, and I had to learn some real lessons in grace.

Prophets are not spared from severe difficulties; rather, they seem to have them more than most. With each difficulty, however, there is a divine expectation to overcome, because every victory is the catalyst for spiritual promotion and genuine increase in authority (see Revelation 2:26). Prophets learn to obey the directives of the Spirit of Christ at any cost, even when they do not understand them. Jesus insists on a posture of humility and instant obedience from His prophets. We speak when He says to speak. We obey when it is not convenient.

Have I mentioned yet the spiritual warfare that prophets endure? This is not the ordinary stuff. This is the kind of warfare that is so personal and ridiculous that one would only talk about it with a few very trusted people. His dealings with all His prophets are very personal and intended to hit the heartstrings. So why would you or anyone endure this? Because it is the only way to experience Him for who He really is and authentically know His ways. Prophets who carry weighty authority do so because they know Him and know Him well.

Different Kinds of Prophets

Earlier I mentioned seer prophets and how there are different kinds of prophets. In the Old Testament, there are three Hebrew words translated into our English word for "prophet" or "seer":

- *Nabi*, the most widely used word for a prophet, comes from a root word that means "'to bubble forth, as from a fountain,' hence 'to utter.'"[4] The following are two examples of *nabi* prophets: "The LORD sent prophets among them to lead them back to him. They warned the people" (2 Chronicles 24:19 NET). "The LORD said to Jeremiah: 'Stand in the gate of the LORD's temple and proclaim this message . . .'" (Jeremiah 7:1 NET).

- *Ro'eh* was introduced in the time of the prophet Samuel and is used seven times to refer to Samuel.[5] We read in 1 Samuel 9:9, "Formerly in Israel, when a man went to inquire of God, he spoke thus: 'Come, let us go to the seer'; for he who is now called a prophet was formerly called a seer." Typically a seer receives prophetic revelation in dreams and visions and can also distinguish the messages of God embedded within creation.

- *Hozeh* also means "seer" (2 Samuel 24:11), which is a synonym of *ro'eh* but a rarer Hebrew term that means "to see" or "to perceive"[6] (as in a vision).

All three words appear in 1 Chronicles 29:29: "Samuel the seer (*ro'eh*), Nathan the prophet (*nabi*), Gad the seer (*hozeh*)."[7]

These three functions have carried over into the New Testament as well. The diversity of New Testament prophets are mostly centered on their *metron* as well as the primary way in which they receive God's voice. A *metron* is a Greek word that means "a measure" or "a limited portion."[8] Frank Damazio, author and former senior pastor of City Bible Church in Portland, Oregon, wrote that the apostle Paul exposed the erroneous way in which ministries self-evaluate by relying on others' measuring rods.

Evaluating themselves by themselves is acting unwisely, and in fact, is harmful. Paul's key ministry concept that he personally

101

lived by is that he knew his "measure," his "rule." Ministry
identity, style, and motives all rest on the understanding of the
ministry *metron*—the sphere God has drawn for you.[9]

Damazio was referring to Paul's words in 2 Corinthians 10:12–18,
especially verse 13: "We, however, will not boast beyond measure,
but within the limits of the sphere which God appointed us."

My husband, Ron, and I are perfectly paired in this regard.
Ron is an apostle, not a prophet, but all fivefold ministers host
a metron as determined by Jesus Christ. Ron's sphere is mostly
regional and includes our city and all of the surrounding cities.
Mine is mostly global, given that I was called as a prophet to
the nations. Ron is not overtly interested in reaching nations,
but he carries an obvious authority for church leadership within
the regional community. I am not overtly interested in regional
outreach, but I target nations strategically with the message that
I carry. Our different metrons are distinctly complementary to
one another's and highly effectual as long as we as individuals
remain primarily within our ministry spheres.

Prophets are given their designated sphere of authority by
Jesus, something He will communicate, confirm and clarify.
They are most effective within that sphere and need to be mindful not to try to operate outside of it. "Most contemporary
prophets believe that their metron stretches as far as their air-
plane tickets," wrote one prophet and author.[10]

> At times, this may be true for national/global prophets, but
> for local prophets it's dangerous to go where you haven't been
> called. Any attempt to minister in an area that you haven't been
> graced or equipped for can subject you to the attack of territo-
> rial spirits in that region.[11]

My experience is that you are never totally immune to such at-
tacks, but there is a marked grace to overcome when you have
stayed within your sphere.

Different spheres include local prophets who are called to build the church locally or are assigned to just one church. Some prophets are called to build one of the "seven mountains of society," which are religion, family, education, government, media, arts and entertainment, and business.[12] Other prophets are assigned to a nation or a cluster of nations. Remember that one sphere is not better than the other. Jesus is the One who calls you, and you are only responsible to Him and not to peer pressure and the mandates of others that appear popular.[13]

What Do Prophets Do?

Ephesians 4:11–12 spells out some overall leadership responsibilities given to all of the fivefold ministers, including the prophets: "He Himself gave some to be apostles, some prophets, some evangelists, and some pastors and teachers, for the equipping of the saints for the work of ministry, for the edifying of the body of Christ." This passage goes on to list the charge to fivefold ministers to promote unity, bring maturity, create stability, speak the truth and expose deceptive doctrines, and cause everyone to become fully functional members of the Body of Christ (see verses 13–16).

Prophets, however, will further engage in a unique set of tasks that flow within their supernatural framework:

1. Prophets call and commission God's next leaders.

Are you aware that all authority on earth comes from God? We read, "Let every soul be subject to the governing authorities. For there is no authority except from God, and the authorities that exist are appointed by God" (Romans 13:1). For that reason, Jesus often works with His prophets to identify, call forth and establish leaders in the earth as He so chooses. The prophet Samuel commissioned Saul as the king of Israel, and later he commissioned David as well (see 1 Samuel 10:1; 16:13). We read in the New Testament that Timothy, the apostle Paul's spiritual son, was commissioned as an apostle through the ministry of a prophetic presbytery. Paul exhorted Timothy with this reminder: "Neglect not the gift that is in thee, which was given thee by prophecy, with the laying on of the hands of the presbytery. Meditate upon these things; give thyself wholly to them; that thy profiting may appear to all" (1 Timothy 4:14–15 KJV). To clarify, a prophetic presbytery is "when two or more prophets . . . lay hands on and prophesy over individuals at a specified time and place."[14] Whether in a presbytery setting or not, prophets call forth God's intended leaders both in the Church and outside of the Church at the word of the Lord. When they do, a supernatural anointing for leadership is released upon the recipients, who are thus spiritually endowed to step into their divine appointments.

2. Prophets give warnings, protect, watch and preserve.

The prophet Hosea reveals to us that a key role of the prophet is to preserve. "By a prophet the LORD brought Israel out of Egypt, and by a prophet he was preserved" (Hosea 12:13). Moses delivered Israel from Egypt, and Moses preserved Israel through his leadership and intercession. Apostle John Eckhardt, author and senior pastor of Crusaders Church in Chicago, wrote, "*Preserve* means to keep from harm, damage, danger, or evil. It also means to protect or save," then added this definition: "In Hebrew, the root word is *shamar*. *Shamar* means to hedge about (as with thorns), to guard, to protect, to watch, and to keep. . . . This word *shamar* emphasizes the protective element of the prophet's mantle."[15]

The prophet Elisha heard the war plans of the enemy king supernaturally and reported back to the king of Israel. Prophets are protective in nature and watch over their assignments in this manner. In 2 Kings 6:8–12 we read,

> Now the king of Syria was making war against Israel; and he consulted with his servants, saying, "My camp will be in such and such a place." And the man of God sent to the king of Israel, saying, "Beware that you do not pass this place, for the Syrians are coming down there." Then the king of Israel sent someone to the place of which the man of God had told him. Thus he warned him, and he was watchful there, not just once or twice.
>
> Therefore the heart of the king of Syria was greatly troubled by this thing; and he called his servants and said to them, "Will you not show me which of us is for the king of Israel?"
>
> And one of his servants said, "None, my lord, O king; but Elisha, the prophet who is in Israel, tells the king of Israel the words that you speak in your bedroom."

Prophets see, hear and feel the encroachment of an enemy supernaturally and will respond accordingly.

This has not changed with God's New Testament prophets. We read how the early Church was saved from a devastating famine because of a prophet.

> And in these days prophets came from Jerusalem to Antioch. Then one of them, named Agabus, stood up and showed by the Spirit that there was going to be a great famine throughout all the world, which also happened in the days of Claudius Caesar. Then the disciples, each according to his ability, determined to send relief to the brethren dwelling in Judea.
>
> Acts 11:27–29

By the prophetic warning of a prophet, the early Church could respond with wisdom and was preserved.

3. A prophet intercedes for people, cities and nations.

All prophets are intercessors. Abraham prayed, Moses prayed, Deborah prayed, Jeremiah prayed and so did all the other prophets. Interceding means "to pray and intervene in favor of another."[16] Some prophets prefer to tear things down. There is a time for this, but prophets who enjoy tearing everything apart have a heart issue. The love of God is not in their hearts. Healthy prophets love to build people and build the Church, not the opposite. Jesus addressed this attitude with His own disciples, who wanted to call down fire from heaven to destroy the Samaritans who rejected their ministry. Jesus rebuked them sternly when He said, "You do not know what manner of spirit you are of. For the Son of Man did not come to destroy men's lives but to save them" (Luke 9:55–56).

The prophetic instructions a prophet receives form the basis of his or her intercession and dialogue with the Lord. The Lord might reveal a present problem or one that is on the horizon. Other times the Lord reveals something new that He is doing. Armed with strategic information, the prophet comes into agreement with God's prophetic word and then speaks it forth in the context of prayer before heaven and earth to establish it.

When the Lord had prepared to destroy Sodom and Gomorrah, He first held a meeting with Abraham about it. The Lord said, "Shall I hide from Abraham what I am doing, since Abraham shall surely become a great and mighty nation, and all the nations of the earth shall be blessed in him?" (Genesis 18:17–18). Then Abraham began to intercede with the Lord for the terms by which to save the two cities if possible. Ultimately, he talked the Lord down to saving Sodom and Gomorrah if ten righteous persons were found in it. There were not ten righteous found, and the cities were destroyed anyway. God is still doing the same today. He is inviting His prophets to intercede for difficult cities and nations because He desires to save them and not destroy them.

4. Prophets proclaim the changes in times and seasons.

To be able to watch over and steward the times and seasons within his or her spiritual assignment, every prophet needs to ask the question, What time is it? The prophet Habakkuk demonstrates this concept, instructing us to write down the prophetic vision, even though it is not for now, but for an appointed time.

> Then the LORD answered me and said: "Write the vision and make it plain on tablets, that he may run who reads it. For the vision is yet for an appointed time; but at the end it will speak, and it will not lie. Though it tarries, wait for it; because it will surely come, it will not tarry."
>
> Habakkuk 2:2–3

God, who sits outside of time, actively works out His purposes throughout history. At the appointed season, He will interrupt chronological time and cause the prophetic vision to become reality.

In the book of Haggai, for example, the remnant Israelites had neglected to rebuild the house of the Lord. They had built their own houses and served their own interests, but neglected the temple and to their material detriment. God then spoke the appointed time to the prophet Haggai. It was time to rebuild. Haggai acted on that word and successfully initiated a new season with the people. The people stepped into the appointed time of the Lord and rebuilt the temple as Haggai stood by encouraging them to be strong and work!

Prophets need to discern the right word for the right time. Ecclesiastes chapter 3 gives us a list of fourteen opposites with an instruction that there is a season and timing for everything. We read a sampling of seasons in verse 2: "A time to be born, and a time to die; a time to plant, and a time to pluck what is planted." What is the point of this passage? The point is, the right word for one season is the wrong word in another season. For example, there are seasons when we are to build and other seasons we are to tear down. In some seasons we are called to fight and other seasons we are to rest. As prophets, then, we are to counsel those who are holding on to their prophetic words past their expiration dates. Prophetic words often have a shelf life and need to be released once the season of their application has passed. Prophets proclaim the new word for the new season, thus providing the Body of Christ with fresh oil and fresh revelation.

As a prophet, how do we know what season it is? The One who holds the key to time is the Holy Spirit, and He partners with His prophets faithfully to reveal what time it is. When He does so, prophets then step into their governing role and release the prophetic word into the platforms they speak into to usher in the change of seasons.

Still, the role of prophets can be as diverse as they are. For example, prophets cry out against unjust systems and structures; they birth new ministries and movements; they demand holiness in God's Church; they are concerned about promoting God's agenda; they inspire and release courage; they are strong discerners and can sense when things are out of order. Prophets also love the truth and will expose deceptions, heresies and lies, which is the topic of our next chapter.

Kingdom Principles

1. Having the gift of prophecy and being a prophet are not one and the same.
2. A prophet is called by Jesus Christ and no one else. If He calls you as a prophet, He will make your calling

abundantly clear. The office of the prophet is also one of the five governing roles in the Body of Christ—apostles, prophets, evangelists, pastors and teachers (see Ephesians 4:11).

3. There are different kinds of prophets. The diversity of New Testament prophets are mostly centered on their *metron*, which is their God-given sphere of authority, as well as the primary way in which they receive God's voice.

4. Prophets and all of the fivefold ministers are charged to promote unity, bring maturity, create stability, speak the truth and expose deceptive doctrines, and cause everyone to become fully functional members of the Body of Christ (see Ephesians 4:12).

5. Prophets will further engage in tasks that flow within their supernatural framework: calling and commissioning God's next leaders; giving warnings, protecting, watching and preserving; interceding for people, cities and nations; and knowing and proclaiming the changes in times and seasons.

Thoughts for Reflection

1. Are you called as a prophet? If yes, how do you know?
2. What are the key differences between having the gift of prophecy and having the call as a prophet?
3. Why are prophets seemingly connected to humble beginnings and great difficulties?
4. If you are a prophet, what kind of prophet are you? A seer? A nabi? And what is your metron?
5. Prophets know the times and seasons. If that applies to you, what time or season is it?

Seven

Stay with Ancient Paths

B randon Showalter, a reporter with the *Christian Post*, interviewed me along with two theologians—Eric Bargerhuff, a professor of theology at Trinity College and professing cessationist, and Dr. Michael Brown, a Messianic Jewish scholar and charismatic theologian—for a controversial news article titled "Can the Chasm between Charismatics and Cessationists Be Bridged? Scholars, Pastors Weigh In."[1] To clarify, a cessationist believes the gifts of the Holy Spirit, such as speaking in tongues, prophecy and healing, ceased with the early apostles, which is a belief system that would deny the reality of most of this book.[2] I was pleasantly surprised to be included in the interview alongside these two highly intelligent men, and in all humor and much like the prophet Amos, I am well aware that I am neither a theologian nor the son of a theologian.[3]

As a Christian prophet and seer who also comes from an occult background, I can offer a knowledgeable and experienced viewpoint about the spiritual realm. And as a functioning pastor in a spiritually vibrant and growing church community, I strive to present this realm with a pragmatic and sensible edge, especially to the prophets and prophetically inclined community. I was not always this way, though. After being delivered from a spirit of sorcery a year after giving my life to Christ, the Holy Spirit gave me an unusually strong anointing for the gift of discerning of spirits—the supernatural ability to distinguish between spirits, either demonic, human or divine. You can read more about this gift, which is one of the nine gifts listed in 1 Corinthians 12:7–10, and about my deliverance in my book *Seeing the Supernatural.*[4]

Long before being called as a prophet, I was operating in the supernatural through a gift of discernment as well as a prophetic gift. All of this was pointing toward an awesome and highly adventurous call into Holy Spirit ministry. In reality, it was extremely hard. Too often I did not understand or know what to do with the spiritual information I had received. I was also having encounters that were deeper and more difficult to process than anyone I knew. In addition, my highly logical husband needed more scriptural support for these prophetic revelations, and my inability to communicate effectively within the framework of his rational, theological mind left me frustrated.

My husband's need for more proof and process, however, was a great blessing in disguise. His need for me to present these concepts in plain language forced me to create a healthy and biblical approach for communication in regard to prophetic revelation, something I insist on from the prophets and prophetic communities that I equip. There is a tendency for prophets to speak too metaphorically and above the heads of most people unless they are made aware of it. I often say to such persons, "Use plain language" and, "Chapter and verse, please."

Eventually I found a large, somewhat organized community of prophets and prophetically gifted persons to connect to, which helped me to grow as a prophet for a season. Prophets and prophetically anointed people need community with like-minded individuals and usually do not thrive on their own. The synergy created in prophetic communities will serve to stir up the Spirit of prophecy and yield sharper, more accurate prophetic words as well as deeper prophetic encounters. And for me, finding a connecting place was an absolute sanctuary—that is, until I noticed the growing amount of theological erosion within the ranks.

At first I was attracted to their beautiful message of God's grace, one of the most powerful messages on grace I have ever heard. Over time, unfortunately, I watched firsthand how this beautiful message would be misapplied to overlook obvious sin. In addition, many core doctrines were being ignored or adjusted within the hearts of those who gathered in this prophetic community, such as the reality of hell, tithing, preaching on sin, spiritual warfare and deliverance, going to church, the biblical narrative for the end times and more. The arguments to reconstruct these core truths sounded revelatory and eloquent, but the fruit of deception was obvious. Adherents grew smug and arrogant in their beliefs, having no obligation to the "institutional" church while becoming lawless in their overall behavior and wholly unsubmitted and unaccountable to any real spiritual authority. Their version of Christianity asserted a "higher" and more "spiritual" prophetic edge, but Jesus gives clear, all-too-often-neglected instructions in Matthew 16:24: "If anyone desires to come after Me, let him deny himself, and take up his cross, and follow Me." Even more concerning was the rampant extrabiblical revelation coming from within that did not serve any practical kingdom purpose other than to gain oohs and aahs from listeners.

Eventually I separated myself from most of this community, being determined to create a company of prophets who were highly supernatural but hosted clear biblical values and the

Spirit's wisdom, which is why I am including this chapter in
this book.

Hyper-Grace Theology

One of the signatures of God's prophets is that they love the
truth and embrace the plumb line of the Word. They demand
an adherence to the Scriptures from themselves and others, especially from other prophets and prophetically anointed people.
When a lie gets into the foundation, however, then all the biblical
boundary lines become altered through the lens of the lie. I like
to point out Proverbs 22:28: "Do not move the ancient boundary
which your fathers have set" (NASB). The context of this verse
is an instruction to leave ancient geographical and property
boundaries in place, but in principle it is an instruction for han-
dling God's Word. We also read, "Whatever I command you, be
careful to observe it; you shall not add to it nor take away from
it" (Deuteronomy 12:32), and several other Scriptures warn us
to not add or take away from His words. With that in mind,
I want to address in this chapter what I believe is the biggest
teaching error attached to the modern prophetic movement,
even though it relates to the gift of prophecy only indirectly.

The grace of God is seen all throughout the Bible and then cul-
minates with the coming of Jesus. The word translated "grace"
in the New Testament comes from the Greek word *charis*, which
W. Vine defined as "'grace,' indicating favor on the part of the
giver, 'thanks' on the part of the receiver, is rendered 'acceptable.'"[5] We can all give one another a measure of grace, but
God's bestowal of grace has a much more powerful meaning.
In His mercy, He gives you blessings instead of cursing you, as
your sin deserves.

I have discovered God's grace to be a perfect covering in
seasons of personal struggle when I felt I was failing the Lord

and people, and I could not yet bring myself together even though I wanted to. His grace, I believe, covers the intermittent gaps of character we all encounter as we journey toward sanctification. At the same time, grace is not a loophole or an excuse for sin or a license to do what Jesus paid with His life to destroy. And this leads us into the discussion of something called "hyper-grace," a very active heresy that has attached itself to many prophetic communities.

The term *hyper-grace* has been used to describe a new wave of teaching that emphasizes the grace of God to the exclusion of other vital teachings, such as repentance and confession of sin. Hyper-grace teachers maintain that all sin—past, present and future—has already been forgiven, so there is no need for a believer to ever confess it.[6] There is also an unnatural reaction toward anything deemed "Old Testament" and "the law." With that, sermons on holiness and the fear of the Lord are often categorized as pharisaic legalism, using such buzz phrases as "Don't judge" and "Love wins" and then asserting that there is no punishment for sin because "God is not an abusive Father." The fruit of this teaching has been the clear erosion of moral boundaries and the veiled leanings toward Christian universalism, which is the view that ultimately all human beings will be "saved" and restored to a right relationship with God.[7] This has shown up as apostasy in certain ministers and other professing Christians who have responded by openly embracing the homosexual lifestyle and blessing homosexual marriages along with other such compromises.

The concept of hyper-grace is not a new one, although the term is. We see the same problem being addressed in the Bible with those in the early Church. Keep in mind that people have always looked for loopholes, even using God's Holy Scriptures out of context to justify their sin. We read, "What shall we say, then? Should we continue to live in sin so that God's grace will increase?" (Romans 6:1 GNT). The apostle Paul here had addressed the obvious error by which people had engaged in licentious sin and then asserted God's grace as some kind of Get Out of Jail Free card to excuse it. He responded, "Certainly not! We have died to sin—how then can we go on living in it?" (verse 2 GNT).

Accused hyper-grace teacher Joseph Prince set the record straight, however, in a *Christian Post* article with Dr. Michael Brown, author of the book *Hyper-Grace*.[8] Joseph Prince is the senior pastor of New Creation Church in Singapore and preaches powerful messages about the grace of God regularly. Prince explained, "If someone is leaving his wife for his secretary and tells you he is under 'grace,' tell this person that he is not under grace but under deception! . . . Genuine grace doesn't compromise God's holy standards and condone sin; it is the answer that gives people power to live glorious lives zealous for good works."[9] In the same article, both Brown and Prince assert that "sanctification is progressive, meaning, the moment we are saved, we are forgiven, declared righteous, and set apart as holy, but now we must grow in holiness."[10]

It is refreshing to see this being discussed and even debated, because the undercurrents of hyper-grace thinking in the modern prophetic movement have neutered much of true prophetic ministry, as far as I am concerned. Many prophetic words now carry the vagueness of the typical horoscope, are lacking in scriptural precedent and then get delivered in a passive communication style with no edge or perceptible anointing. Furthermore, such instructors have drilled into their prophetic communities that personal prophecy is strictly for edification, exhortation and comfort, which is scripturally true,[11] yet neglects other New Testament Scriptures that clearly stretch prophetic ministry beyond that criteria. Again, if there is a lie in the foundation, then everything comes under that distortion, and so prophetic words are often adjusted or neglected to fit the hyper-grace paradigm rather than to reflect the heartbeat of the Holy Spirit.

A fire chief spoke to me at my church regarding one of his firefighters, who had lost his daughter in some kind of accident. (She was not a believer in Christ.) As he spoke, I had a vision of a woman standing unclothed in a prison cell in the depths of hell. The vision lasted about half a second, but I saw that she was in her late twenties with dark hair to her waist. I also felt hell's unbearable heat and became quite disturbed and desperate once I experienced it. Keep in mind that I had never met this woman or her family, yet my description of her to the fire chief was spot-on. In desperation, I begged him to find a way to get me inside the morgue so I could attempt to raise her from the dead. I had no idea if I would be able to accomplish that or not.

Unfortunately, my request went unanswered, but even more disturbing were the comments from a guest minister at our church that same day. He was a semiknown healing revivalist, but one who held all the associations of those ministers immersed in hyper-grace theology before I understood what all of this was. When I communicated this story to him, his response was, "Aww! Don't worry! She'll be just fine!" I thought his response was totally ridiculous but did not make the connection until years later that either he did not believe in hell or he did not believe that hell was a permanent fixture for those who reject Christ. This is what skewed his response to the spiritual vision.

Do you remember Dr. Dave Williams from chapter 4? At a conference, Dr. Williams shared candidly with our church about the time he was rebuked prophetically. "I was planning my revenge," Dr. Williams said. "Someone did something to me, and I was going to humiliate him back." Dr. Williams added that he was on autopilot with his anger, and though he was a pastor, he still did not realize what he was doing at the time. Then he received a phone call from the late prophet Dick Mills. "I have a word from the Lord for you: 'Repent!'" Dr. Williams knew what this was in reference to and adjusted himself instantly.[12] Realize that prophetic ministry in the hyper-grace circles would have never condoned this kind of prophetic word. It would have been "harsh" and "condemning" and "not the heart of the Father." Yet arguably, it was the right prophetic word for that moment and exactly what Dr. Williams needed to hear.

No prophet or prophetically gifted person who carries the Father's heart enjoys or wants to deliver a harsh word to someone. Regardless, love always rejoices in the truth,[13] and that intense love of the Father will compel you at times to prophesy a necessary word to intervene in a wrong action or decision. This same prophet gave Dr. Williams another powerful prophetic word, only much later, when he said, "I have a word from the Lord for you. You will become a powerful financial deliverer." This, too, was a right prophetic word, just like the other one, and Dr. Williams now has a thriving, successful ministry dedicated to creating millionaires and multimillionaires who are connected to the Great Commission.[14]

Next, I will address some of the most common excesses and errors involving the gift of prophecy that we need to be aware of.

Excesses in Prophetic Ministry

As with all supernatural ministry, the gift of prophecy comes with its own set of excesses, misunderstandings and wrong application. This is the human element attached to a perfect gift from the Holy Spirit that always has to be evaluated and addressed. Here are some of the most common:

Prophetic manipulation

You might be asking how it is even possible for the prophetic and manipulation to go together, which leads us to a very candid discussion about the anointing and having a clean heart. One definition of manipulation is "to control or play upon by artful, unfair, or insidious means especially to one's own advantage."[15] Given its accessibility, a downside is that the gift of prophecy is not distributed by the Spirit based on merit. Once you have the prophetic gift, the Holy Spirit does not revoke it either. People become anointed with this gift but are still in the process of personal sanctification. Unfortunately, there are some who, having perpetually unresolved issues with greed, power, lust, etc., remain stuck in that process and misuse the gifts of the Spirit to advance their selfish agenda.

Prophetic manipulation can manifest in many different ways. I remember the ministry partner who threw this one on me: "I know things about you that you don't know that I know." I knew she was inferring that the Holy Spirit had showed her secret things about me that were most likely negative. I waited for her to elaborate, only she never did, even when I asked her to. Later, when I brought it to her again for some kind of explanation, she had an ugly, emotional reaction, and the issue never did get resolved. Her statement was a prime example of prophetic manipulation and a tactical move to gain power by suggesting she knew a secret about me. This is also a form of emotional blackmail and borderlines on prophetic bullying.

Another woman, a popular author and prophet, had a secret struggle with prescription painkillers. She could be a hilarious teacher of the Word and also minister prophetically with a deep impact and unusual accuracy. Sadly, her prophetic gift became the perfect deception for her drug abuse, as she could discern the medical professionals in the audience and then work her story to them so as to convince them to prescribe her prescription painkillers. Remember that God does not let these things go on forever, but they often go on a lot longer than any of us are comfortable with. When I found her high on painkillers during a conference at my church, I initiated the uncomfortable confrontation, and she never spoke to me again.

Prophets and prophetically anointed people have to examine their heart motives constantly. You may have a right prophetic word from the Holy Spirit, but your delivery might turn into manipulation when there are unchecked or unhealed heart wounds. Sometimes we do not even know that an evil agenda is at work within us, such as what Dr. Williams experienced. With that said, can I exhort you once again to pray what I pray every day over myself? I ask the Holy Spirit to "create in me a clean heart" (Psalm 51:10), because I know I am just as susceptible to deception and wrong motives as anyone else is. Being a part of a healthy church community that will lovingly confront you when needed and then routinely visiting reputable inner healing and deliverance counselors will prove helpful.

Charging money for prophetic words

For most, charging money for prophetic words is a black-and-white issue and something that should never, ever be done. I do not do this myself, and most prophets that I know do not do it either. Still, we see in the Old Testament that people would bring to the prophet a monetary gift in exchange for prophetic ministry, something which, depending on context, was not considered wrong. For example, we read in 1 Samuel 9 how Saul and his servant had gone to inquire of the prophet Samuel about their lost donkeys and had a discussion on the way about what gift they should give Samuel for his supernatural help. If you are familiar with Middle Eastern culture, and my husband comes from this culture, then you would recognize this to be a gesture of honor and not a bribe. In much of the Body of Christ, however, we love to starve our ministers and prophets, yet insist they produce on demand. On the flip side, there are prophets who have a greedy heart and misuse their anointing and office for financial gain, which the Lord hates.

I have encountered a few select individuals who function as legitimate "prophet-consultants." These are prophets who charge a fee or retainer for access to their prophetic ministry and are often sought out by the business community or those who need a higher caliber of prophet to interact with. Still, it is always best to operate from a place of mutual honor. A prophet should not have to request a fee, and the recipient of the prophet's ministry should know to be generous and to honor the anointing. It is because we do not understand honor that we even have these kinds of arrangements, which are arrangements that should be understood as the biblical and cultural norm rather than something negotiated.

Divination disguised as prophecy

Just to reemphasize, the gift of prophecy is a supernatural ability from the Holy Spirit that will clarify the heart and mind of God in a situation, reveal what is concealed or declare the future. There are many other religions and spiritual practices that claim to do the same, but without any heart connection to the Holy Spirit, any use of the name of Jesus or any consideration of the written Scriptures. We would refer to this as *divination*, which is defined as "the art or practice that seeks to foresee or foretell future events or discover hidden knowledge usually by the interpretation of omens or by the aid of supernatural powers."[16] The Bible is clear that we are not to participate in any kind of divination and considers it idolatry, which would include the reading of horoscopes, astrology, palm reading, tarot cards, ouija boards, reading tea leaves, consulting psychics or the use of any other magical method to see the future. Usually these practices are obvious to the Bible-believing Christian, but divination has since disguised itself as the gift of prophecy in many charismatic circles for another largely undetected reason.

When Moses went up the mountain to be with the Lord, the Israelites coerced Aaron, their acting priest and Moses' brother, to create a gold calf to worship in his absence. Aaron complied, and thus they reverted back to the hideous pagan-style revelry they had left behind in Egypt. When Moses learned of their grievous sin, he left the mountain to deal with them, and their penalty was deadly. The Levites began executing the rebellious idolaters, and the Lord released a plague against them. The worst part came next when God told Moses He would send His angel ahead of them to drive out the enemy tribes from their Promised Land, but that He would not go with them. Moses understood that their protection and blessing came from the abiding presence of the Lord, and that His presence distinguished the Israelites from every other race on earth. Moses could not tolerate this, and he interceded boldly, saying, "If Your Presence does not go with us, do not bring us up from here" (Exodus 33:15). What we learn here, however, is that it is possible for you and me to step into God's promises without any sense of His presence, and this happens often.

Again and again, I have watched people in prophetic churches and communities prophesy without any real connection to His presence. At best, their spiritual-sounding words come from their own imagination and are discernable as such. At worst, they have now bargained with another spirit, specifically a spirit of divination, to produce the prophecy, which is not as easy to detect unless you are very discerning. The slave girl with the spirit of divination in Acts 16 spoke by demonic revelation, but what she said was true. She said about Paul and his companions, "These men are the servants of the Most High God, who proclaim to us the way of salvation" (verse 17). Paul discerned her words as coming from a demon, and he cast it out.

Unchecked selfish motives and agendas, performance mentalities, jealousy and competition within prophetic communities are all open doors for a spirit of divination to come in and operate instead of the Spirit of God. Being in vital friendship with the Holy Spirit is a thrilling yet challenging lifestyle by which He takes aim to eradicate every insecure, unsubmitted and unclean tendency within your own heart, which purifies the prophetic word as it flows through you. Despite these challenges, Moses showed us how to cultivate a powerful connection with His presence. He did this by going back to God again and again in authentic friendship until he transformed and visibly radiated with His presence. You and I are being challenged to learn that kind of connection with the Spirit, what keeps it and what breaks it. When you prophesy in union with Him, your prophetic words will reflect His transformational anointing. They will be accurate and carry the felt resonance of eternity.

Extrabiblical revelations

Lone prophets with highly mystical edges are the most prone to extrabiblical revelations. When I say that someone is mystical, what I mean is they are typically more experiential in their spirituality and are often characterized by uncommon beliefs and revelation. Being mystical is not necessarily bad, except when your spiritual teachings and beliefs are extrabiblical. And surprisingly, there are always those few who succeed in gathering followers and fellow ministers to these crazy teachings.

A prophet in New Zealand has asserted interesting claims about the spiritual realm as well as special knowledge of an extraterrestrial realm. "This teacher claims to have created galaxies, travelled to distant planets and uncovered sinister plans of fallen alien races that are hell-bent upon corrupting human DNA for their own nefarious purposes," wrote Australian prophet and author Phil Mason.[17] Mason added that "he presents himself as a deeply mystical figure who knows far more than he is permitted to publicly disclose" and claims to be seated on a "Galactic Council" and mentored by invisible beings.[18] Several of us became more familiar with the controversial New Zealand prophet after his teachings were presented by then protégé Jason Westerfield at a controversial gathering in California in 2015. Westerfield was a former ministry school student and "son of the house" at Bethel Church in Redding, California. After the gathering, he was publicly rebuked by Bill Johnson, senior leader of Bethel Church, for the heresy.[19]

Another fairly well-known prophet in Europe suggested in a podcast that we become a generation of higher wisdom, which includes living a "gospel" of life and immortality. He expounded on several Scriptures that refer to the promise of life in God and in Christ but explained them to mean that you and I can cheat death once we have a higher revelation. His inference throughout the podcast was clear. He proposed that enlightened believers will not physically die and can become immortal. He also believes there will not be a "bad end times" because that is a mentality of death. Once again, this is an example of extrabiblical revelation that uses pet Scriptures while leaving out the contradictory Scriptures, such as "It is appointed for men to die once, but after this the judgment" (Hebrews 9:27), and then twists other verses to prove their preferred spiritual philosophy.

I think you are getting the point. When it comes to prophetic excess and strange revelations resulting in even stranger doctrines, my husband has said many times, "There is nothing new under the sun." Heresies today are pretty much the same heresies yesterday, and a historical understanding of such heresies, especially Gnosticism,[20] will help you to identify them as they emerge and reemerge.

In dealing with excesses, however, there is a tendency to become jaded and suspicious in regard to prophetic ministry. We are exhorted by the apostle Paul to "not despise prophecies" and in the same breath to "test all things; hold fast to what is good" (1 Thessalonians 5:20–21). Realize that God will never confine His voice to our finite language or to our ideals in regards to prophetic ministry. He is fully expressive and engages us with deeper and more meaningful discourse as we mature in Him. With that, there will always be a certain amount of tension as we sift through the myriad of prophetic revelation to sort out what is God and what was the pizza someone ate the night before. He is speaking His secrets and distributing His wisdom, which then implies a protocol to process and communicate what He is revealing.

Kingdom Principles

1. God's prophets love the truth and embrace the plumb line of the Word. When a lie gets into the foundation, however, then all the biblical boundary lines become altered through the lens of the lie.

2. Hyper-grace theology has been used to describe a new wave of teaching that emphasizes the grace of God to the exclusion of other vital teachings, such as repentance and confession of sin. The fruit of this teaching has been the clear erosion of moral boundaries and even apostasy in certain ministers and other professing Christians.

3. Hyper-grace thinking in the modern prophetic movement has neutered much of true prophetic ministry. Many prophetic words now carry the vagueness of the typical horoscope, are lacking in scriptural precedent and then get delivered in a passive communication style with no edge or perceptible anointing.

4. Prophets and prophetically anointed people have to examine their heart motives constantly. You may have a right prophetic word from the Holy Spirit, but your

delivery might turn into manipulation when there are unchecked or unhealed heart wounds.

5. Selfish motives and agendas, performance mentalities, jealousy and competition within prophetic communities are all open doors for a spirit of divination, the counterfeit to the prophetic, to eventually come in and operate instead of the Spirit of God.

Thoughts for Reflection

1. Can you explain the differences between grace and hyper-grace? How does God's true grace treat sin?

2. How has hyper-grace thinking impacted prophetic ministry that you know of? Or has it not affected it?

3. Are you intentional about checking your heart motives when it comes to prophetic ministry? Are there people in your life whom you trust who will help you to see any blind spots?

4. Are you aware of the presence of the Holy Spirit in your life? How about when you prophesy? Can you describe or define your connection with the Spirit of God?

5. Are you given to more mystical expressions of the gift of prophecy? How do you guard yourself from extra-biblical teachings and revelations?

Eight

Wisdom for Visions, Dreams and Signs

The night before ministering at a Sunday church service in Australia, I had a disturbing dream. In the dream, I was in someone's home and experienced the agony of injustice and the tension of false accusations. I had also discerned a demonic spirit had stirred up some people into making the allegations. Also in the dream, out of stubbornness I refused to be silenced and only became louder.

I woke up very early that morning fully energized but with thoughts rolling around in my spirit: *Do you have a fight in your heart? You don't back up, you rise up!* And, *Destinies long held captive are being set free*. In summary, I knew from the dream and my subsequent thoughts that something beyond difficult had gone on in that church and in the lives of the attendees, it was deeply spiritual and I was to minister to this somehow. Only I did not quite know how.

Later that day, I attended the pre-service prayer meeting with some of their core intercessors just before the Sunday service began. Originally, I had prepared a heartfelt message about cultivating a relationship with the Holy Spirit and how to carry His glory. (To clarify, the glory of God is the supernatural and visible manifestation of God's presence and something you can read more about in my book *Glory Carriers*.) I expected that we would experience His tangible glory in the church service since I flow in that message and ministry with regularity. As we prayed together, my spiritual eyes opened to see with unusual clarity into the spiritual realm.

In my vision, I saw two angels who looked like men but shone brightly with the glory of God. They were the purest glistening white in their faces, hair, clothing and overall appearance. And they were interacting with each other as if they were having a planning discussion. One angel—I discerned by the Holy Spirit he was there for "glory"—appeared then to yield his lead to the other angel, who had been sent on assignment to "restore time." As I watched all of this, I felt in my spirit that the Holy Spirit was knitting together the beginnings of a powerful deliverance and restoration for this church and those in attendance. I needed to change my overall direction and instead minister from the contents of the dream and the vision.

At the afternoon church service, I addressed the key points from the dream and what came into my thoughts afterward. Then I explained the unusual angelic interaction and invited those in attendance to stand up in their seats if what I said applied to them. I said something like this: "If you feel as if you have lost time because you were stuck in a contention, if your destiny and purpose has since been held captive, then stand up. I want to pray for you." After people stood to their feet and I prayed over them, a wind seemed to sweep through the meeting space. As part of this unusual manifestation of the supernatural, those who stood for ministry began to shake and moan right in their seats. This angelic encounter proved to be both powerful and pivotal. A ministering spirit, sent by God in response to their prayers, had been officially released.[1] We read in Hebrews 1:7, "He sends his angels like the winds, his servants like flames of fire" (NLT). This angel was sent to restore lost and stolen time across the spectrum of this church, and those who stewarded this moment properly would enter into a divinely ordered catch-up season.

Understand that if you are going to minister or operate effectively out of a dream, a vision or some other kind of spiritual happening, there is a process attached to it. *Process* is defined by one dictionary as "a series of actions or operations conducing to an end."[2] Again, prophetic wisdom is what escorts us through the process that accompanies all prophetic revelation into fruition. This is not human wisdom, but a wisdom that comes from the Holy Spirit. Thankfully, I was well prepared after years of these kinds of experiences to process this kind of dream and unusual vision of the two angels with swiftness and accuracy, although that is not always typical. Usually I have to take more time, depending on the complexity of what is being revealed. Either way, my process began immediately with prayer, specifically asking for the Holy Spirit's wisdom about the dream, as well as insight into my subsequent thoughts spooling immediately after.

Typically, the first question we ask when interpreting dreams is, "Who is the dream about? Is the dream about you or about someone or something else?" Even though I was in the dream and experiencing all the elements of the dream, it was not about me. I knew in my spirit the dream was about this church. You might be asking next, "How, exactly, did you know that?" I perceived it by how the dream was weighted. Simply put, I did not feel that red-hot danger signal I would have felt if the dream had been directly for me. This point of interpretation has developed from repeated personal experience, however, thus making it more of a guideline and not an overall rule for dream interpretation.

Either way, it felt more like traveling through someone else's journey, and I was learning the important details as if I experienced it myself. As a result, I knew from the dream that there had been a contentious battle and discerned the demonic source behind it and its assignment to silence this church. In the dream and in my subsequent thoughts, I also understood God's intended plan. He had purposed to give them their fight back and to give them their sound back. With that, I began to pray into God's intended outcome in preparation to hear His wisdom, directives and next steps as He revealed them.

Simple Tips for Interpreting Dreams

Do you have dreams at night? If so, I want to tell you without a doubt that you, too, are having dreams from God. More dreams than not are spiritually sourced, which is a truth that we dismiss because our dreams are often nonsensical to our rational minds. And a dream from the Lord is always a beautiful invitation from Him for dialogue, something I find fascinating. Dream language, by the way, is a higher language and requires some level of working out in order to lay hold of its interpretation. That is why your dreams are commonly steeped in metaphors and symbols that are not readily understood, rather than in plain language. How, then, can you extract a genuine spiritual interpretation from the hodgepodge of scenes and images that play out on the screen of your mind in the night? Solid dream interpretation necessitates a season of study from solid, reputable Christian dream experts.[3] Interpreting dreams is not something you can to try to figure out flippantly by googling keywords or looking at random sources. We can, however, start somewhere, and listed below are some quick tips to help you get started with simple dream interpretation.[4]

1. Who is the dream about?

Most of the time, the dream is about you, and you are the action hero in the dream, with other people involved in different ways. Something is happening or about to happen, and you are being given the heads-up by the Holy Spirit so you can pray intelligently. Other times, you are in the dream, but only as an observer or a standby figure. When you are the observer or standing by, often you are being shown something needful, only it is about someone else or an external situation. This is something you always take first to God in prayer for His counsel. Negative dreams about other people, most of the time, should never be discussed outside of the prayer closet. It is extremely unfair and unnerving to assassinate someone's good character or to vocalize impending harm or death to someone or about someone, all based on a dream.

2. Is it a good dream or a bad one? Does it repeat?

I love the good dreams and am comforted, encouraged and hopeful when I have them, but what about the bad ones? And what about the bad ones that repeat themselves? Remember that negative dreams could also be demonically sourced, and the Holy Spirit will reveal that to you if you ask Him. We take authority over the projected evil outcomes of such dreams in Jesus' name and render them useless against our lives. On the other hand, negative dreams could also be God's personalized warning system to us so we can pray effectively to avert something coming or to pray in order to get the very best outcome out of something unavoidable. The repeating dreams, however, might be about something needing resolution or God's voice to you that you cannot avoid something coming and to prepare yourself. All such dreams are an invitation to find out more from the Holy Spirit, and it is important to take that step and really listen to His counsel.

3. What are the main facts of the dream?

The prophet Daniel had a variety of intense dreams and visions, and he processed them by writing them down, but only "the main facts" (Daniel 7:1). Dreams often have so many symbols and scenes that you cannot possibly process and interpret them all, and they do not contribute to the overall meaning of the dream anyway. For simple interpretation, you will want to focus on just three or four of the most important details and then set the rest to the side. For example, I once had a dream that I killed two black widow spiders on a sunny day in the backyard of the home that I grew up in. These were the main points of the dream and the basis for my interpretation. I ignored the other miscellaneous details because they were just dream "noise" in my opinion and did not need my attention. (By the way, this dream meant that I had effectively dealt with two areas of generational occultism.)

4. What area of your life is the dream about?

Is the dream about your family, your work or your ministry perhaps? Knowing what area of your life is being addressed in the dream will narrow down the interpretation and application and help you to respond with more precision. The meaning of the dream will have application, then, for just that area of your life rather than for your life overall. For example, when I had dreamt about being in someone's home, but not my home, I coincided the timing of the dream with the church gathering I was preparing for. Since a house can symbolize a church, I concluded the Holy Spirit was pointing to something going on with this fellowship that He wanted to remedy. I did not presume an action plan, however, but waited on Him to reveal prophetic wisdom.

Again, this is a very simple step-by-step interpretation process that I hope will guide you into a basic understanding of what your dream could mean. I do encourage you to resource yourself further with materials from reputable Christian experts and to avoid the secular or new age ones. If dream interpretation methods are not biblically based, you will not arrive at the proper interpretation and will totally miss God's dream directives for your life.

Angelic Involvement

Have you ever seen or dreamt about angels? What should you do or not do when this happens? The second phase of this prophetic revelation involved the vision of the two angels.

In the early Church, believers saw and encountered angels frequently, which means that we have the potential to experience the same. I do not doubt that people see and encounter angels from time to time. What they do with the spiritual information often concerns me, however, when their interpretations are not joined with wisdom. By the way, seeing or discerning the angels is an operation of the Holy Spirit's gift of discerning of spirits.[5]

I have studied angelic involvement quite thoroughly, so I engaged a quick mental search through the written Word just to make sure that what I saw and concluded were congruent. When it comes to angels, it is critical to have a solid biblical understanding about the workings of these mighty beings, or your interpretation and application will be in error. To create a baseline of understanding, here are some points to consider:

1. Angels have been sent to help us.

Angels are the heavenly sanctioned administrators of God's many blessings for His people. "What are the angels, then? They are spirits who serve God and are sent by him to help those who are to receive salvation" (Hebrews 1:14 GNT). Angels help us in the following ways and so many more:

- Protection (see Daniel 6:20–23; 2 Kings 6:13–17)
- Guidance (see Mark 16:5–7; Acts 8:26)

- Strength (see 1 Kings 19:5–8; Daniel 10:10; Luke 22:43)
- Revealing information (see Luke 1:11–20; Acts 1:9–11)
- Provision (see Genesis 21:17–20; 1 Kings 19:5–7)
- Arriving in response to prayer (see Daniel 9:20–23; Acts 12:5–12)
- Fighting demonic spirits (see Daniel 10:20; Revelation 12:7)
- Caring for believers upon death (see Luke 16:22; Jude 9)

Even if you do not particularly see them, the Bible shows us that there are an "innumerable company of angels" (Hebrews 12:22), legions of them (see Matthew 26:53) and thousands upon thousands of them (see Daniel 7:10). There is no shortage of angelic help.

2. Angels are God's messengers.

The Hebrew word for "angel" is *malak*, meaning "messenger."[6] Consider that not only do angels *speak* a message as He permits them to—they *are* a message. An angel spoke of four future kingdoms to Daniel; an angel spoke to Zachariah about his wife's miracle conception; and an angel told Philip where to travel so as to find the salvation-seeking Ethiopian eunuch.[7] When Jacob dreamt, he heard the voice of God and watched the angels ascend and descend between heaven and earth. "How awesome is this place!" he said. "This is none other than the house of God, and this is the gate of heaven!" (Genesis 28:17). And an angel stirred the waters at the pool of Bethesda as a message to the onlookers to come to the water and be healed (see John 5:4).

Likewise, when I saw the glory angel concede his lead to the other angel, I saw the heavenly message and adjusted my direction accordingly. Once we have tested the vision for congruency with the written Word and have understood its general message, we can cooperate with it. For example, an angel directed Joseph in a dream to take Mary as his wife, and he cooperated with the heavenly instruction (see Matthew 1:18–24). And an angel opened the prison doors so the apostles could go free, then instructed them to go and preach the Gospel to those at the temple, a command the apostles obeyed (see Acts 5:17–20).

3. Angels do not replace Jesus.

Angels represent Jesus, but do not take His place. In other words, we are not to get caught up in the worship of angels or to become overly fascinated with them. The apostle Paul warned the Galatians to not entertain an angelic messenger with a message contrary to the Gospel (see Galatians 1:8). He also urged the Colossians to guard themselves from being defrauded by those who worship angels (see Colossians 2:18). When the apostle John fell down and falsely worshiped at the feet of the angel, the angel rebuked him immediately: "See that you do not do that! I am your fellow servant, and of your brethren who have the testimony of Jesus. Worship God! For the testimony of Jesus is the spirit of prophecy" (Revelation 19:10).

4. Angels are tasked with specific assignments.

Just to name a few, Michael the archangel protects Israel specifically (see Daniel 12:1). God gives His angels the authority to protect us personally (see Psalm 91:11) and even assigns angels to children (see Matthew 18:10). In Revelation chapters 2–3, we see that an angel is assigned to the church of a specific city and that Jesus might even communicate His instructions, at His choosing, to these angels through His designated representatives, in this case John the apostle.[8]

When we align correctly with the message of the messengers, then we have aligned to God's heavenly mandates simultaneously, thus creating the heaven-to-earth connection.

Communicating the Revelation

The distinct challenge I faced with this dream and vision was knowing how to communicate something this intangible, but in a pragmatic and applicable way. If I did not communicate with wisdom, my words would come across as highly mystical and lacking in any real spiritual substance. *How do I establish that there is an angel here to "restore time"? How do I communicate the unusual restoration that God has prepared for them in a convincing way?* This was quite a mental jump and would require that I include a point-by-point discussion about the supernatural dimensions of time and what God is able to do with it. As with the topic of angels, I have also studied the flexible nature of time. Again, I did a quick mental search through the Scriptures to try to recall everything I could in regard to what God does with time.

First of all, time is something that God created for mankind, but is not confined to Himself. We read about this in Genesis 1:3–5: "Then God said, 'Let there be light'; and there was light. And God saw the light, that it was good; and God divided the light from the darkness. God called the light Day, and the darkness He called Night. So the evening and the morning were the first day." Although we are subjected to time, God is not. This might explain how "with the Lord one day is as a thousand years, and a thousand years as one day" (2 Peter 3:8). It also explains references to events that took place before the foundation of the world, such as being chosen by Christ, His works having already been completed and the Lamb being slain—all of which played out in chronological time and yet were finished beforehand.

We also read about when Joshua commanded time to stand still so he could complete his battle mission against the Amorites. He said before the Lord and the Israelites, "'Sun, stand still over Gibeon; and Moon, in the Valley of Aijalon.' So the sun stood still, and the moon stopped, till the people had revenge upon their enemies" (Joshua 10:12–13). Here, time was extended for Joshua and the armies of Israel for divine purposes. This shows us that time is bendable and something that can be shortened, sped up and restored as needed. Hopefully now you are catching my point behind God's plan to restore some lost time—that it is entirely possible in His Kingdom.

I explained these concepts to this congregation as best I could, then prayed for those in need. We read how the Lord will confirm His word with signs and wonders following (see Mark 16:20). The encounter that followed with an angelic wind going throughout the room helped to prove my authenticity, something I am grateful for. I have also taken note that, like Jesus, we can ask our heavenly Father to send us angelic help for the things we know that angels do (see Matthew 26:53). If time has been stolen from you, I want to encourage you to ask our heavenly Father for an angel to be sent on assignment to restore it. Time is a kingdom commodity and something God will bend, shorten, quicken, lengthen and restore for His divine purposes.

Communicating a prophetic revelation from God requires that we communicate with clarity both His message and His heart. This is especially challenging when a prophetic revelation emerges through highly symbolic dreams, visions, angelic visitations, signs and more. With that said, here are a couple of guidelines to help you:

1. Make the message plain.

In Habakkuk 2:2, God instructs His prophet to "write the vision and make it plain on tablets, that he may run who reads it," because this vision was for intended for others, not just for Habakkuk. It had to be written down in clear, plain language, therefore, to be easily understood by those who would read it.

This concept is reinforced in the New Testament in 1 Corinthians 14:7–9 with regard to the Holy Spirit's gift of tongues and interpretation. If the sound is without distinction, it will render people unable to prepare for battle. In this context, the spiritual gift of tongues needs to be joined with an interpretation from the Holy Spirit. Without the interpretation, the utterance in tongues is not useful or edifying to the hearers.

I have been privy to many prophets and their various prophetic communications, both verbally and in written form. I have noticed the blessing of some prophets who not only prophesy but also know how to teach. These prophets, who also instruct, know instinctively how to make the message plain and memorable to listeners and readers. On the other hand, there are others who prophesy, only you have no idea what they are saying. I have taken note that they are definitely anointed and their words sound exciting. Unfortunately, the overuse of mystical language and ambiguous concepts causes the prophecy to get lost in the translation or to be misunderstood. Their message is not plain, so you cannot run with it the way God intends.

If this is your bent, be prepared then to explain your symbols more thoroughly and to clarify your metaphors, citing biblical passages and reputable resources. Do the work beforehand to bring forth a prophetic communication that has clarity.

2. Take adequate time for process.

Prophetic words are weighted differently depending on their context. There are heavier words and then there are lighter words, depending on what the Holy Spirit is initiating. If you are from an older Pentecostal or charismatic expression, you will recall that it was common for people to engage in spontaneous prophecy. In other words, they would stir up the gift of prophecy and then prophesy by faith[9] by opening their mouths and saying whatever spilled out. Nowadays, we see a similar function but in its next-generation form. We see this spontaneous expression in the form of prophetic teams, namely organized groups of men and women who are anointed by the Spirit to prophesy. Prophetic teams are typically utilized during church services and conferences, for personal ministry, in Christian outreaches and in many other contexts. The prophetic words that emerge from this format are usually lighter, albeit accurate, and typically framed as words of edification, exhortation and comfort to the recipient (see 1 Corinthians 14:3).

For the weightier words, you have to take more time with it. These are words that come out of dreams or trances typically, and the anointing on them is noticeably heavy. Something or someone is going to shift, as these kinds of prophetic words do not leave their recipients the same way as they came. We take more time to process them to make sure the interpretation is congruent with written Scriptures, that our pride or our wounds are not coloring the word and that we have the Father's heart when we communicate. One prophetic teacher said this:

> Many prophetic people don't understand that the most commonly recognized Hebrew word for prophecy, "naba—bubbling up," refers primarily to the way of receiving prophetic revelation, not of giving it. So they receive a bubbling up of revelation, open their mouth and let it spill out, often without any processing before they speak.[10]

A word can be lost or misrepresented when we do not take the time to process it.

Once I had a vision concerning a popular full-time itinerant minister. My husband and I knew him personally, and he had ministered at our church several times. It was a very simple vision that played out like a quick movie right in front of me. I watched him walk into a house, and I could feel a new partnership forming with this residence. I was sure the vision meant he was to leave itinerant ministry to pastor a church, something I brought first to the Lord in prayer. As it turned out, the Holy Spirit never did permit me to say anything to him, and so I did not. Several months went by before I received news that this minister had been offered an assignment, not to pastor a church but to write a book for a popular publishing house. I am so glad I did not say anything, because I had wrongly interpreted the vision! Taking the time to process prophetic revelation prevented me from giving him wrong information. It also saved me some embarrassment.

Processing prophetic revelation also sifts through deceptive emotionalism that can disguise itself as prophecy. For example, when the State of New York legalized the gruesome third-trimester abortion law, I watched one popular prophet release a written word of judgment against America that he believed to have received through a vision. He compared a particular idolatrous nation in the Bible to America, then proceeded to illustrate God's pending judgment on this nation unless we repent of abortion. Given the timing, I believe his prophetic word was in reaction to New York State's new law and needed more processing. First of all, the new law was endorsing what had already been happening behind closed doors in the state for several years. Third-trimester abortions were not new, only now they were legal.[11] If the word had been released beforehand, like just before the law was signed, I might have paid more attention. It came right after, however, which is why I believed it to be emotive and reactive.

Also, I could not reconcile how the collapse and destruction of America by an angry God would fix the problem. The writing took direct aim at Christians not doing enough to eradicate abortion both prayerfully and legislatively, but neglected to address the foretold end time ministry of Elijah, which would reknit the hearts of children to their fathers and fathers to their children (see Malachi 4:5–6). We are in this generation now, and his prophetic word came across to me as coming from an Old

Testament framework. Lastly, to proclaim judgment against an entire nation for any reason would require tremendous humility on the part of the prophet. Personally, I would not be able to release that kind of word without great fear and trembling and much personal repentance beforehand.

We are all going to make mistakes from time to time when it comes to prophetic revelation. We might interpret something incorrectly, prophesy before we have processed the revelation thoroughly enough, or flat-out get it wrong. If you want to have grace for your mistakes, then have a teachable spirit and maintain a posture of humility at all times. Be quick to apologize for your errors, but in this manner: If you said it privately and in error, correct it privately. If you said it publicly and in error, correct it publicly. Finally, make sure you put in place a mechanism for feedback and theological pushback if needed if you plan to grow in communicating prophetic revelation with impact.

❀❀❀❀

As I conclude this book, *Prophetic Secrets*, I am excited about releasing the road-tested keys and prophetic wisdom that I have accumulated and taught for more than twenty years. My heartfelt prayer is for this book to activate you in the prophetic with power—not only activate you, but also anchor you to His Word and lead you to apply the principles of sound interpretation for visions, dreams and spiritual happenings. For centuries, the Holy Spirit hinted prophetically that this day would come. You have now emerged in fulfillment of the prophecy, "Your sons and your daughters shall prophesy" (Joel 2:28).

This is my prayer for you:

Holy Spirit, I invite You to empower those reading this book with a greater measure of Your prophetic grace. Give them eyes to see and ears to hear what You are saying. Speak to them in dreams, through visions and in creation.

Allow them to grow in compassion and prophetic accuracy. Make them a prophetic conduit for those all around them who need to know that You see them and know them personally. I pray this gift would yield salvations and a harvest of souls throughout the globe. I pray this gift would build Your Church and edify Your people. I pray for Your prophetic anointing to bring these hungry readers and listeners a sense of nearness to You through an intimate knowing of Your heart. In Jesus' name, Amen.

Kingdom Principles

1. If you are going to minister or operate effectively out of a dream, a vision or some other kind of spiritual happening, there is a process attached to it.
2. Dream language is a higher language and requires some level of working out in order to lay hold of its interpretation. That is why your dreams are steeped in metaphors and symbols rather than in plain language.
3. More dreams than not are spiritually sourced, which is a truth that we dismiss because our dreams are often nonsensical to our rational minds.
4. Angels come in response to our prayers. They are God's messengers and are sent to us to fulfill specific assignments. It is normal, not abnormal, to see them at times. The Holy Spirit might have us share with others what the angels are doing.
5. When communicating prophetic revelation, even if it came to you through an extraordinary way, we are to make the message plain and understandable to others. We should not speak so mystically or metaphorically that it goes above the heads of most people.

Thoughts for Reflection

1. How would you know if a dream is from God or not? And then how would you know if it is just for you or for someone else?

2. Have you ever seen an angel? Why did you see it? What was it there for?

3. Have you ever tried to communicate prophetic revelation to others based on a dream or vision before? Were you able to explain what you experienced or saw with clarity, or did you feel inadequate to explain it?

4. Can you discern the difference between heavier prophetic words and lighter prophetic words? How would you know the difference?

5. Have you ever communicated a prophetic word incorrectly (either it was not a prophetic word after all, or you misinterpreted it)? How did you handle your mistake?

Appendix

How to Stir Up the Gift
of Prophecy

The young Timothy was exhorted by Paul, his apostle and spiritual father, to "stir up the gift of God which is in you through the laying on of my hands. For God has not given us a spirit of fear, but of power and of love and of a sound mind" (2 Timothy 1:6–7). Apparently you can have a supernatural gift, and for the purposes of this book the gift of prophecy, but your gift can go dormant unless you keep it alive and activated.

What does it mean, then, to stir up your gift? One Greek to English translation wrote it this way: "For which reason I remind you to fan into flame the gift of God, which is in you through the laying on of my hands."[1] The Greek word for "stir up" is *anazōpyréō*, which means "to kindle anew, rekindle, resuscitate."[2] It also appears from the text that a spirit of fear, which is a demon, will attempt to quench your supernatural gifts if you submit to it. As we fan the gift of prophecy into full flame, we will need to step into faith and overcome any feelings of fear.

Through your study and reading of this book, you have already stirred up the gift of prophecy. Here are just a few more of the many ways to stir up the gift of prophecy: reading about the topic, listening to audio teachings and messages, being in or visiting prophetic environments and prophetic training courses, and revisiting personal prophetic words or words given through others. And below I have included some simple activation exercises to support you as you stir up the gift of prophecy. These are creative ideas that you can bring to the Holy Spirit at any time and ask Him to breathe on for the purposes of personal prophecy:

1. Prophesy to body parts.

Different body parts in the Bible symbolize different things. With a variety of Scriptures in hand, you can prophesy to different parts of the body as the Holy Spirit leads you and release powerful words as you prophesy.

- *The mind.* He is renewing you "in the spirit of your mind" (Ephesians 4:23)! Every argument, every lie is cast down from your mind; your thoughts are obedient to Christ (see 2 Corinthians 10:5). You have "the mind of Christ (1 Corinthians 2:16), and you have been given the spirit of wisdom and revelation" (Ephesians 1:17).

- *The eyes.* "Blessed are your eyes for they see" (Matthew 13:16). You will see marvelous things; your eyes are being opened to see His law (see Psalm 118:23; 119:18). You will see mysteries unveiled in the visions of the night (see Daniel 2:19).

146

- *The ears.* Your ears are attentive to wisdom, and you have the ears of the wise (see Proverbs 2:2, 18:15). Your ears are blessed "for they hear" (Matthew 13:16), and you will hear what the Spirit is saying to the churches (see Revelation 3:22).

- *The shoulders.* He is granting you great strength upon your shoulders. You are a leader and you carry a governmental anointing. He is removing the heavy burdens off your shoulders, the burdens He did not author. These burdens will be removed far away from you (see Isaiah 9:6; 14:25).

- *The back.* God has your back! His glory will be your "rear guard" (Isaiah 58:8); He will "go before you" and protect you from behind (52:12); He will lift you in every place you have been bowed down and lost strength to stand (see Psalm 145:14).

- *The legs.* You will "run and not be weary"; you will "walk and not faint" (Isaiah 40:31); You are a finisher! You will finish your race and not be cut short (see 1 Corinthians 9:24–27).

- *The feet.* Now is the time to take your inheritance. Every place you put the sole of your foot will be yours (see Joshua 1:3–8). He makes your feet "like hinds' feet" and sets you on "high places" (Psalm 18:33).

2. Prophesy using objects.

We see in the Bible that occasionally the prophets would illustrate their prophetic words using objects. For example, the prophet Agabus took hold of Paul's belt and bound his own hands and feet with them to warn Paul that the Jews would bind him and deliver him to the hands of the Gentiles (see Acts 21:10–11). Here are some possibilities to consider. Wait on the

Spirit to see or hear if anyone is a candidate for the following objects and prophetic words. Or explore other objects and co-inciding Scriptures.

- *A pen.* Your tongue is "the pen of the ready writer" (Psalm 45:1). It is time to write; it is time to speak. You "will write the vision and make it plain" (Habakkuk 2:2). Write the book! Start the blog! Do the podcast!
- *A watch.* The Lord is calling you to be a watchman in prayer (see Ezekiel 3:16–17). You will "watch and pray" (Matthew 26:41). You will watch with impact.
- *Change.* Your season is about to change (see Ecclesiastes 3). The Lord is doing "a new thing" (Isaiah 43:19). What you thought would not change is changing.
- *A key.* You have been given the "keys of the kingdom" (Matthew 16:19). Use your keys; use your spiritual authority. You have the keys for this! What you open no one will shut; what you shut no one will open (see Isaiah 22:22).
- *A phone.* You are "called according to His purpose"; everything is working out for your good (Romans 8:28). You have a holy call, and an upward call (see 2 Timothy 1:9; Philippians 3:19).

3. Prophesy back all the things that are lost.

God is the great restorer of lost things. His "gifts and callings . . . are "irrevocable," and "all things work together for good" for those who love Him (Romans 11:29; 8:28). Not only does He seek and save the lost, but He restores our covenant blessings that have been stolen from us. Is the Holy Spirit showing you an area of loss in someone's life that needs to be restored? If so, prophesy into it and take back what was lost.

- *Lost time.* He is restoring to you all the lost years that were eaten up (see Joel 2:25); He is restoring "everything you lost" (Deuteronomy 30:3 MSG).

- *Lost dreams.* God has not changed His mind about you. He says to begin again: "The old is gone, the new has come" (2 Corinthians 5:17 GNT). His power is working in you; He can "do superabundantly more than all that we dare ask or think [infinitely beyond our greatest prayers, hopes, or dreams]" (Ephesians 3:20).

- *Lost wealth.* He will give you a "double portion" for what was lost (Isaiah 61:7). The Lord says the thief is caught! You will receive a sevenfold payment back to you (see Proverbs 6:31).

- *Loss of peace.* God has not given you a spirit of fear, but of power, love and a sound mind (2 Timothy 1:7). You are pleasing to the Lord, and He makes even your enemies live in peace with you (see Proverbs 16:7). You "both lie down in peace, and sleep" (Psalm 4:8).

- *Loss of health.* He is "the LORD who heals you" (Exodus 15:26); He "heals all your diseases" (Psalm 103:3). By His stripes you are being healed right now (see 1 Peter 2:24).

4. Prophesy based on the color that you see.

This is an exciting activation for those who are beginning to see in the spiritual realm. Colors have biblical meanings, so you can ask the Holy Spirit to show you a color, and then based on the meaning of the color, you can prophesy to someone what the Holy Spirit is saying.

It helps first to know both the positive and negative meanings of colors. Here is a list of such from Autumn Mann's "Biblical Dream Dictionary."[3]

Meanings of Colors in Dreams

Color	Positive Meaning	Negative Meaning
Black	Death, mystery	Sin, darkness
Blue	Revelation, communion	Depression, sorrow, anxiety
Brown	Compassion, humility	Compromise, humanism
Gold/amber	Purity, glory, holiness	Idolatry, defilement, licentiousness
Gray	Maturity, honor, wisdom	Weakness
Green	Growth, prosperity, conscious	Envy, jealousy, pride
Orange	Perseverance	Stubbornness
Pink	Childlike, love of God	Childishness
Purple	Authority, royalty	False authority
Red	Wisdom, anointing, power	Anger, war
Silver	Redemption, grace	Legalism
White	Righteousness, holiness	Religious spirit
Yellow	Hope, mind	Fear, cowards, intellectual pride

Let's say that you see the color red in your spirit in connection with someone. You will want to ask the Holy Spirit if you are seeing that color for a positive or negative reason, as well as what area of his or her life you are to prophesy into. For example, if He is addressing power in that person's life, then you might be led to prophesy strengthening words over him or her, such as "He gives power to the faint and increases the strength of the weak" (Isaiah 40:29 BSB). There is really no formula to follow, but this is generally how you would engage in this kind of activation.

You can also fan the gift into flame by joining with like-minded Christians and engaging in intentional prophetic activation exercises with them. I challenged one of my online mentoring groups, for example, to give a Scripture-based prophetic word to someone within a week's time and to tell the group their results. They did a great job overcoming fear and stepping out in this prophetic activation, some for the first time. I also challenged them to give one another prophetic words in our Facebook group, which was very powerful and encouraging.

What about you? Now that you have learned the language of heaven and received the Spirit's anointing, it is time to begin prophesying. You will be amazed at the words and images that will emerge from heaven's throne. Demonstrating to others what God sees and knows about them—that He loves them blissfully and has unique plans for their abundant future—will prove to be an incredible experience. And I know that He will meet you as you step out in faith. Are you ready to heed His call?

Notes

Introduction

1. The LDS Church appears similar to Christianity on the surface but is very different in its theology underneath. You can read about those differences in the appendix of my first book, *The Intercessors Handbook* (Minneapolis: Chosen, 2016), or my blog post titled "The Key Differences Between Christians and Mormons (Latter-Day Saints)," April 20, 2017, https://www.jennifereivaz.com/2017/04/20/the-key-differences-between-christians-and-mormons-latter-day-saints/.

2. David R. Seely, "Prophecy," *The Encyclopedia of Mormonism* (New York: Macmillan, 1992), quoted in BYU Library, https://eom.byu.edu/index.php/Prophecy.

3. Mormons believe we pre-existed in heaven prior to being born on the earth. They also believe in eternal families, past and future. Eternal families are marital unions in heaven that produce children. In the LDS belief structure, God the Father had a beginning, and so did Jesus Christ. Jesus was titled the firstborn Son because he was born first. Eventually He became a god because of His good works. They believe the rest of us were born in like manner as Jesus, and through good works we can also become a god in much the same manner.

4. According to the denomination's website (https://www.upci.org/about/about-the-upci), the United Pentecostal Church

> emerged out of the Pentecostal movement that began with a Bible school in Topeka, Kansas, in 1901 and with the Azusa Street Revival in Los Angeles, California, in 1906. It traces its organizational roots to 1916, when a large group of Pentecostal ministers began to unite around the teaching of the oneness of God and water baptism in the name of Jesus Christ.

5. You can read more about receiving the baptism of the Holy Spirit in the appendix of my book *Glory Carriers* (Minneapolis: Chosen, 2019).

Chapter 1 Discovering the Gift of Prophecy

1. The "Spirit of glory" is another name for the Holy Spirit (1 Peter 4:14).

2. Sam Storms, "What Does Scripture Teach about the Office of Prophet and the Gift of Prophecy?," *NIV Zondervan Study Bible*, ed. D. A. Carson (Grand Rapids: Zondervan, 2015), quoted by The Gospel Coalition, October 8, 2015, https://www.thegospelcoalition.org/article/sam-storms-what-does-scripture-teach-about-office-prophet-gift-prophecy/.

3. "4394. prophéteia," *Strong's Concordance*, Bible Hub, https://biblehub.com/greek/4394.htm.

4. "4395. prophéteuó," *Strong's Concordance*, Bible Hub, https://biblehub.com/greek/4395.htm.

5. Sam Storms, "Why NT Prophecy Does Not Result in 'Scripture-Quality' Revelatory Words (A Response to the Most Frequently Cited Cessationist Argument Against the Contemporary Validity of Spiritual Gifts)," SamStorms.com, November 4, 2013, https://www.samstorms.com/enjoying-god-blog/post/why-nt-prophecy-does-not-result-in-scripture-quality-revelatory-words-a-response-to-the-most-frequently-cited-cessationist-argument-against-the-contemporary-validity-of-spiritual-gifts (site discontinued).

6. This is often called the prayer of "impartation" and implies the divine ability of someone to give, share or bestow what he or she has to another person, typically through the laying on of hands.

Chapter 2 Prophetic Words Need Prophetic Wisdom

1. "God, who at various times and in various ways spoke in time past to the fathers by the prophets . . ." (Hebrews 1:1).

2. "Pursue love, and desire spiritual gifts, but especially that you may prophesy" (1 Corinthians 14:1).

3. "What Does the Bible Say About Muslims/Islam?," Bibleinfo, https://www.bibleinfo.com/en/questions/what-does-bible-say-about-muslims-islam; "Is the Arab Nation Descended from Ishmael?," CBN, http://www1.cbn.com/online/discipleship/is-the-arab-nation-descended-from-ishmael%3F.

4. Wisdom is referred to as "her" in Proverbs 3:13–18.

5. "Wisdom," Lexico, https://en.oxforddictionaries.com/definition/wisdom.

6. "G4678—sophia," *Strong's Greek Lexicon* (KJV), Blue Letter Bible, https://www.blueletterbible.org//lang/lexicon/lexicon.cfm?Strongs=g4678&t=kjv.

7. Rick Renner, "A Spirit of Wisdom and Revelation for You," Rick Renner Ministries, January 21, 2017, https://renner.org/spirit-of-wisdom-and-revelation-for-you/.

8. "G601—apokalyptō," *Strong's Greek Lexicon* (KJV), Blue Letter Bible, https://www.blueletterbible.org//lang/lexicon/lexicon.cfm?Strongs=g601&t=kjv.

9. Renner, "Spirit of Wisdom and Revelation."

10. Eivaz, *Seeing the Supernatural* (Minneapolis: Chosen, 2016), 99.

11. For more on this topic, see my book *Seeing the Supernatural*.

12. Harvest Church, "Sunday Morning | Mario Murillo," YouTube video, December 3, 2018, 00:29:47, https://www.youtube.com/watch?v=ypEZ07vlWPg&t=2401s.

13. "Mario Murillo," YouTube video, 00:38:52.

14. "What Is a Parable?," Got Questions Ministries, https://www.gotquestions
.org/what-is-a-parable.html.

15. Eivaz, *Intercessors Handbook*, Kindle edition, 71–72.

Chapter 3 Perceiving the Prophetic Word

1. "The next day, as they went on their journey and drew near the city, Peter went up on the housetop to pray, about the sixth hour. Then he became very hungry and wanted to eat; but while they made ready, he fell into a trance and saw heaven opened and an object like a great sheet bound at the four corners, descending to him and let down to the earth" (Acts 10:9–11).

2. "And He who sat there was like a jasper and a sardius stone in appearance; and there was a rainbow around the throne, in appearance like an emerald" (Revelation 4:3).

3. Various translations of this verse have lent to various interpretations. For example, some translations end this verse more as a question than an action by saying, "Should I be enquired by them at all?" More traditional commentaries suggest God's "answer" to these inquiring idolaters to be a highly punitive one. The interpretation I have presented is one I have heard taught in several pulpit settings. It presents idolatry as first being an issue with the heart, and heart issues are what blind us to the prophetic voice of God.

4. "Behold, I send the Promise of My Father upon you; but tarry in the city of Jerusalem until you are endued with power from on high" (Luke 24:49).

5. Derek Prince, "The Laying on of Hands: Imparting Blessing, Authority and Healing," *The Teaching Legacy of Derek Prince*, DPM Archive XVI, no. 1, 1, https://www.derekprince.org/Publisher/File.aspx?id=1000021532.

Chapter 4 The Spirit of Wisdom

1. Dave Williams, "My Astonishing Vision: Part 1," Dave Williams Ministries, June 3, 2018, https://davewilliams.com/my-astonishing-vision-part-1/.

2. Dave Williams, "My Astonishing Vision: Part 2," Dave Williams Ministries, June 11, 2018, https://davewilliams.com/my-astonishing-vision-part-2/.

3. "Indeed He says, 'It is too small a thing that You should be My Servant to raise up the tribes of Jacob, and to restore the preserved ones of Israel; I will also give You as a light to the Gentiles, that You should be My salvation to the ends of the earth'" (Isaiah 49:6).

4. See Galatians 2:11–14.

5. Chris Oyakhilome, *The Seven Spirits of God*, SmashWords ed. (LoveWorld Publications, 2006), Kindle edition, chapter 2.

6. The Holy Spirit's weighty glory came upon them and affected their physical mannerisms temporarily as they spoke out the praises of God miraculously in languages they could not possibly have known beforehand. Some of the witnessing crowd were astonished and believing, but others accused them of being drunk. By the unction of the Holy Spirit, Peter spoke out in their defense and explained how

this was not actual drunkenness, but the outpouring of the Spirit in fulfillment of Joel's prophecy (see Acts 2:1–21; Joel 2:28–29).

7. James Goll, "Do You Know the Seven Spirits of God?," YouTube video, August 28, 2017, 00:36:45, https://www.youtube.com/watch?v=tmX0ohBNA8Q.

8. "G4678—sophia," *Strong's.*

Chapter 5 Anointed to See

1. "What Is the Second Heaven?," Got Questions Ministries, https://www.gotquestions.org/second-heaven.html; "The Three Heavens – Q&A With Pastor John Hagee," *JOY! Digital*, https://www.joydigitalmag.com/burning-issues/the-three-heavens-qa-with-pastor-john-hagee/.

2. Patricia King, "The Seer Anointing with Jamie Galloway // Supernatural Life // Patricia King," YouTube video, https://www.youtube.com/watch?v=KRt-oZUQJ58&t=487s.

3. Ruth Heflin, *Glory—Experiencing the Atmosphere of Heaven* (Hagerstown, Md.: McDougal Publishing, 1999), 191–193.

4. Joel Osteen, "Meditate on God's Word," Joel Osteen Ministries, https://www.joelosteen.com/Pages/Article.aspx?articleid=6487.

Chapter 6 Wisdom and Secrets for Prophets

1. Diane Lake, "Do You Know Why Fivefold Ministry Is Essential?," Generals International, October 12, 2015, https://www.generals.org/articles/single/do-you-know-why-fivefold-ministry-is-essential/.

2. Ibid.

3. J. Lee Grady, "Can You Spot a Prophet?," *Charisma Leader,* August 31, 2004, https://ministrytodaymag.com/152-archives/fivefold-ministries/9654-can-you-spot-a-prophet.

4. M. G. Easton, "Prophet," *Easton's Bible Dictionary*, Bible Study Tools, https://www.biblestudytools.com/dictionary/prophet/.

5. Ibid.

6. John W. Ritenbaugh, "Bible Verses about Hozeh," *Forerunner Commentary*, BibleTools.org, https://www.bibletools.org/index.cfm/fuseaction/topical.show/RTD/cgg/ID/9214.

7. "Prophet," *Easton's Bible Dictionary*, http://www.freebiblecommentary.org/special_topics/prophet.html.

8. "3358. metron," *Strong's Exhaustive Concordance*, Bible Hub, https://biblehub.com/greek/3358.htm.

9. Caleb Juarez, "Your Metron by Frank Damazio," *A Word for the Season* (blog), June 14, 2016, https://thirdheavenrealities.blogspot.com/2016/06/your-metron-by-frank-damazio.html.

10. Larry Randolph, *User Friendly Prophecy: Guidelines for the Effective Use of Prophecy* (Shippensburg, Penn.: Destiny Image Publishers, 1998), Kindle edition, chapter 10.

11. Ibid.

12. "The Seven Mountains of Societal Influence," Generals International, https://www.generals.org/rpn/the-seven-mountains/.

13. This section, "Different Kinds of Prophets," was previously published as Jennifer Eivaz, "What Type of Prophet Are You?," The Elijah List, November 19, 2019, https://www.elijahlist.com/mobile/display_word.html?ID=22836.

14. Bill Hamon, *Apostles, Prophets, and the Coming Moves of God* (Shippensburg, Penn.: Destiny Image Publishers, 1997) Kindle edition, chapter 6.

15. John Eckhardt, *Prophet, Arise* (Lake Mary, Fla.: Charisma House, 2015), 132.

16. Eivaz, *Intercessors Handbook*, Kindle edition, 38.

Chapter 7 Stay with Ancient Paths

1. Brandon Showalter, "Can the Chasm between Charismatics and Cessationists Be Bridged? Scholars, Pastors Weigh In," *The Christian Post*, March 20, 2018, https://www.christianpost.com/news/can-chasm-between-charismatics-cessationists-be-bridged-scholars-pastors-weigh-in.html.

2. "Cessationism," Theopedia, https://www.theopedia.com/cessationism.

3. Amos, unlike most prophets, was a herdsman and farmer by trade and then summoned by the Lord to prophesy (see Amos 7:14). "An interesting biographical touch. Prophecy, like other occupations, tended to form a hereditary guild, but Amos was not by birth a prophet" (*Ellicott's Commentary for English Readers*, https://biblehub.com/commentaries/amos/7-14.htm).

4. To better understand how the demonic can operate in believers, see my blog article "Can A Christian Be Demon Possessed?," https://www.jennifereivaz.com/2017/11/28/can-a-christian-be-demon-possessed/. This article also appears in the appendix of my book *Seeing the Supernatural*.

5. W. Vine, "Accept, Accepted, Acceptable," *Vine's Expository Dictionary of New Testament Words*, Blue Letter Bible, June 24, 1996, https://www.blueletterbible.org/search/Dictionary/viewTopic.cfm; see also "G5485—charis," *Strong's Greek Lexicon* (KJV), Blue Letter Bible, https://www.blueletterbible.org//lang/lexicon/lexicon.cfm?Strongs=G5485&t=KJV.

6. "What is Hyper-Grace?," *GotQuestions.org*, https://www.gotquestions.org/hyper-grace.html.

7. Stoyan Zaimov, "Christian Universalism 'Alive and Well' and Must Be Opposed, Says Modern Christianity Professor," *The Christian Post*, July 3, 2018, https://www.christianpost.com/news/christian-universalism-alive-and-well-must-be-opposed-modern-christianity-professor-michael-mcclymond.html.

8. Michael Brown, *Hyper-Grace: Exposing the Dangers of the Modern Grace Message* (Lake Mary, Fla.: Charisma House, 2014).

9. Michael Brown, "Hyper-Grace: Setting the Record Straight with Pastor Joseph Prince," *The Christian Post*, January 30, 2017, https://www.christianpost.com/news/hyper-grace-setting-the-record-straight-with-pastor-joseph-prince.html.

10. Ibid.

11. "He who prophesies speaks edification and exhortation and comfort to men" (1 Corinthians 14:3).

12. Dave Williams, "Wealthy Place Seminar" (seminar, Harvest Church, Turlock, Calif., September 27, 2019).

13. "Love . . . does not rejoice in iniquity, but rejoices in the truth" (1 Corinthians 13:4, 6).

14. Williams, "Wealthy Place Seminar."

15. "Manipulate (*vb.*)," *The Merriam-Webster.com Dictionary*, https://www.merriam-webster.com/dictionary/manipulate.

16. "Divination (*n.*)," *The Merriam-Webster.com Dictionary*, https://www.merriam-webster.com/dictionary/divination.

17. Phil Mason, *The New Gnostics, Discerning Extra-Biblical Revelation in the Contemporary Charismatic Movement* (Byron Bay, Au.: Quantum Ministries Ltd, 2019), 116.

18. Ibid., 116–117.

19. Darren Wilson, "Bill Johnson Publicly Rebukes Popular Prophetic Voice," *Charisma News*, https://www.charismanews.com/opinion/behind-the-lens/49490-bill-johnson-publicly-rebukes-popular-prophetic-voice. I also knew someone who attended the Westerfield gathering in Redding and was able to detail its aftermath.

20. The heresy of Gnosticism threatened to destroy the early Church. Its core attributes were "the thought and practice especially of various cults of late pre-Christian and early Christian centuries distinguished by the conviction that matter is evil and that emancipation comes through gnosis" ("Gnosticism (*n.*)," *The Merriam-Webster.com Dictionary*, https://www.merriam-webster.com/dictionary/gnosticism). Gnosis is the "knowledge of spiritual mysteries" (https://www.lexico.com/en/definition/gnosis). Phil Mason's book on the topic provides understanding as to how this has shown up in the modern charismatic movement.

Chapter 8 Wisdom for Visions, Dreams and Signs

1. "Then he said, 'Don't be afraid, Daniel. Since the first day you began to pray for understanding and to humble yourself before your God, your request has been heard in heaven. I have come in answer to your prayer'" (Daniel 10:12 NLT).

2. "Process (*n.*)," *The Merriam-Webster.com Dictionary*, https://www.merriam-webster.com/dictionary/process.

3. I spent a year focused on dream language and interpretation and enjoyed learning from sources written and produced by these top Christian dream experts and others: John Paul Jackson, Doug Addison and Jane Hamon.

4. I have readapted these four simple steps for dream interpretation from Doug Addison's book *Understand Your Dreams Now* (InLight Connection, 2013).

5. For more on this topic, see my book *Seeing the Supernatural*.

6. "4397. malak," *Strong's Exhaustive Concordance*, Bible Hub, https://biblehub.com/hebrew/4397.htm.

7. See the book of Daniel; Luke 1:13; Acts 8:26.

8. Eivaz, *Seeing the Supernatural*, Kindle edition, 104–105.

9. "Having then gifts differing according to the grace that is given to us, let us use them: if prophecy, let us prophesy in proportion to our faith" (Romans 12:6).

10. Lyn Packer, "How to Communicate a Clear Written Prophetic Word," New Zealand Prophetic Network, https://www.nzpropheticnetwork.com/how -to-communicate-a-clear-written-prophetic-word-by-lyn-packer.

11. Based on a discussion about the availability of third-trimester abortions with a long-term pastor from New York City who had attended Harvest Church in Turlock, Calif. This conversation took place a few years before the law was passed.

Appendix How to Stir Up the Gift of Prophecy

1. William D. Mounce, "2 Timothy 1:6," *Mounce Reverse-Interlinear New Testament*, https://www.biblegateway.com/passage/?search=2+timothy+1%3A 6&version=MOUNCE

2. "G329—anazōpyreō," *Strong's Greek Lexicon* (KJV), Blue Letter Bible, https://www.blueletterbible.org/lang/lexicon/lexicon.cfm?t=kjv&strongs=g329.

3. Autumn Mann, *Unlocking Your Dreams: A Biblical Study Manual for Dream Interpretation* (CreateSpace, 2015), in "Biblical Dream Dictionary," Unlocking Your Dreams, http://www.unlockingyourdreams.org/dream-dictionary/; "Colors," Unlocking Your Dreams, http://www.unlockingyourdreams.org/dream -dictionary/colors/.

Jennifer Eivaz is a minister and international conference speaker with a heart to equip the Church in the supernatural and for raising up passionate and effective prayer. She is a regular contributor to Charisma Online and The Elijah List, has been featured on several Christian television shows, hosts the popular podcast *Take Ten With Jenn* and has authored several bestselling books. Jennifer lives with her husband, Ron, and their two children in Turlock, California, where she serves as an executive pastor at Harvest Church.

To find out more about Jennifer and her ministry, you can visit her online:

Website: www.jennifereivaz.com
YouTube: Jennifer Eivaz
Facebook: www.facebook.com/jennifereivaz/
Twitter, Periscope and Instagram: @PrayingProphet

Harvest Church
225 Fourth Street
Turlock, CA 95380
www.harvestturlock.org

More from Jennifer Eivaz

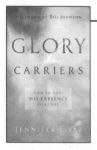

The glory of God is irresistible. Yet to only seek experiences of it is to miss the point. His glory is the natural outpouring of a deep relationship with the Holy Spirit. In these pages, you'll discover how to enter into an intimate fellowship with the Spirit of God, step into the supernatural, carry His glory to the darkest places and see His kingdom come.

Glory Carriers

The gift of discerning of spirits is the powerful, supernatural ability to hear and see into the spiritual realm. Yet it's often overlooked and misunderstood. Full of real-world application, this essential, foundational guide shows how you can sense, discern and battle in the spiritual realm, expose the hidden threats and help lead the way to victory.

Seeing the Supernatural

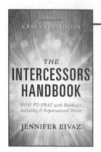

Many Christians turn to prayer with open hearts, but seldom get the answers they seek. Why? Sharing stories of her own breakthroughs, Eivaz offers much-needed direction and biblical context for prayer that makes a difference. Learn how to navigate the spiritual realm of prayer with authority and confidence by using the tools that make it truly effective.

The Intercessors Handbook

✔Chosen

Stay up to date on your favorite books and authors with our free e-newsletters. Sign up today at chosenbooks.com.

 facebook.com/chosenbooks   @chosen_books

 @Chosen_Books